THE MALTESE ISLANDS

THE MALTESE ISLANDS

CHARLES OWEN

FREDERICK A. PRAEGER, *Publishers*

New York · Washington

BOOKS THAT MATTER

Published in the United States of America in 1969
by Frederick A. Praeger Inc., Publishers
111 Fourth Avenue, New York, N.Y. 10003

Library of Congress Catalog Card Number: 70-90677

PRINTED IN GREAT BRITAIN

To my mother

CONTENTS

ILLUSTRATIONS

ILLUSTRATIONS

*Photographs not otherwise acknowledged
have been supplied by the Tourist Board
in Valletta*

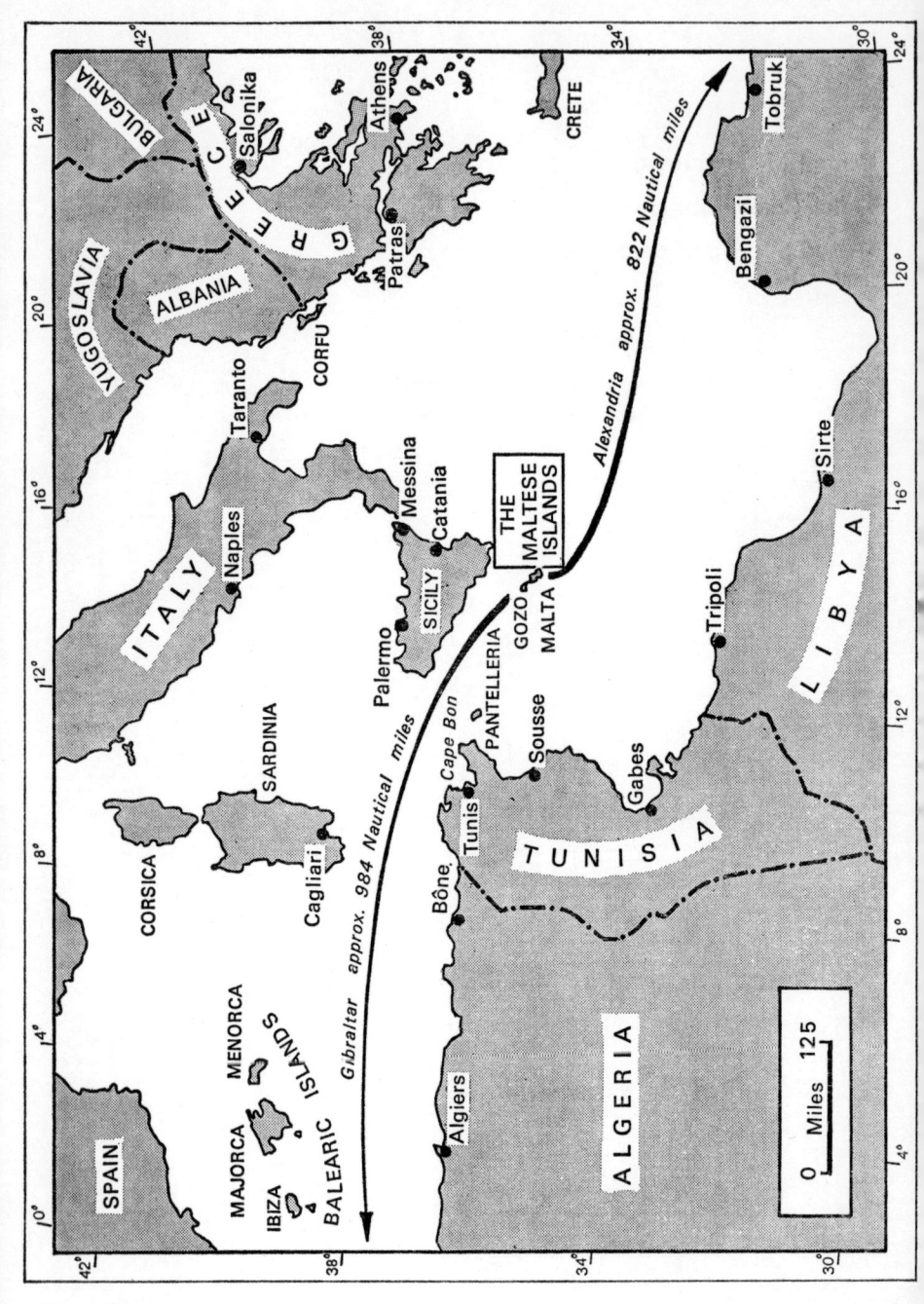

1   AT FIRST SIGHT

IF first impressions matter, the Maltese Islands are best approached by ship. From seaward, as the main island and the harbour breakwater take shape, the unfolding scene is dramatic.

Valletta, the islands' capital, rises theatrically out of the water, with its tiers of neat houses and dignified buildings above massive ramparts, a pale golden tapestry set in the brilliant blue of sky and sea. Across Grand Harbour from Valletta, deep-water creeks shape and divide the ancient cities of Vittoriosa and Senglea, each poised serenely upon its promontory. The main port, steep-sided, impregnable, a glorified moat, is lively with shipping, and its quays with people and their traffic; while, high above the bustle, onlookers gaze down from terraced gardens and watch discerningly the berthing of the newly-arrived ship. The harbour vistas, with their strong flavour of history, reminiscent of Venice but loftier, sterner, less fragile, are among the finest of their kind in the world.

The islands, for the most part, do not look very interesting from the air. The modern visitor, approaching Luqa in his jet, sees briefly a rather featureless countryside, unbroken by mountains, forests or rivers. In the winter or spring, there stretches below him a pattern of green and brown terrain divided by bleak stone walls; in the summer the parched landscape looks uniformly dun, bare and rocky.

As country gives way to town, he becomes aware of spreading, close-packed cities, with Valletta conspicuous on its high peninsula, centrepiece of a jigsaw of fawn land and blue water. The aircraft approaches the runway; there is a jumbled impression of church towers, battlements, rectangular buildings, flat roofs, busy

13

roads; and as his plane comes to rest, the simple unpretentious airport claims him.

There is a pleasant air of informality at Luqa and one of the prime Maltese characteristics, the welcoming smile, is quickly evident. The airport is close to the built-up surroundings of Valletta and, as the visitor is driven towards the capital, he will be reminded that he has arrived in a country with one of the highest population densities in Europe. He will also become aware that, while signs of the colony still linger, this is a distinctive nation, with a unique culture, language and racial characteristics.

The Maltese tends to be short in stature, stocky, swarthy, sturdy in gait, with a relaxed but dignified bearing. His country having been occupied through the centuries by a succession of foreign powers, he has acquired a cosmopolitan outlook and a tolerant attitude to visitors. Besides his own language, he speaks English; he is likely also to speak Italian and, if the product of a high school, French or Latin. He is an unmistakably Mediterranean species but less volatile than his neighbours, warm-hearted but not demonstrative, articulate but patient, gentle, wise and self-assured.

The Maltese language is Semitic, originally a Punic dialect, influenced strongly by the Arabs during their domination of the islands, with gleanings of Romance vocabularies, mainly Italian, and further accretions through widespread religious and cultural connections. It became a written language only in recent times, making use of Roman characters adapted for the interpretation of Arabic sounds. It is a puzzling language; for example, the letter *c* may be pronounced hard as in cat or *ch* as in church, the letter *g* hard as in goat or *j* as in jackal, *h* is sometimes silent and at other times aspirated, *j* as *y*, and *x* as *sh*. Even the simplest courtesies have their pitfalls. The Maltese for yes is *iva*, for no is *le*, for please is *jekkjoghbojk*, for left is *xellug*, for right is *lemin*, and so on. Until the visitor has mastered the pronunciation of

place names—such as Marsaxlokk, Mgarr, Qrendi and Siggiewi
—his touristic ambitions may be somewhat frustrated.

LOOKING FURTHER

After entering the city gate the first impression of Valletta may
be disappointing. The main street, Kingsway, is flanked for much
of its length by small undistinguished shops, many of them offering supplies and souvenirs aimed at sailors and tourists. But it
requires only a little effort of exploration to discover that Valletta
is a gem among small cities, its straight streets leading always
towards a glimpse of the blue sea, widening out here and there into
shady squares flanked by the splendid palaces and public buildings bequeathed by the Knights of the Order of St John of Jerusalem. There are tranquil patios, fine houses with ornamental
balconies, and dignified churches.

Valletta carries itself like a major metropolis and, after a while,
the visitor comes to realise that it is indeed a complete microcosm,
impeccably to scale, of a capital city many times its size. From its
numerous vantage points, each offering panoramic views of great
beauty, the visitor appreciates that he is in a land of considerable
extent and surprising visual variety, far-reaching but always inti-
mate, a neat complex of all the activities that make up a nation's
life, each in its own place, the whole blended together into a
coherent pattern.

The Maltese Islands—known generally by the main island's
name, Malta—are an archipelago comprising the main island, the
smaller sister island of Gozo, the islet of Comino and two large
rocks, Cominetto and Filfla. Some 320,000 people live there. Of
these, about 295,000 inhabit the main island, and, apart from a
few dozen on Comino, the remainder are Gozitans. Most industry and the chief centres of trade and education continue to be
located on the main island, Gozo being a largely agricultural community, and over one-third of the total population lives in the

15

Valletta-Sliema area (map p 113). By size of population the principal cities and towns are Sliema (25,000), Valletta and Birkirkara (18,000 each), Hamrun (16,000) and, with fewer than 15,000 each, Qormi, Rabat, Zejtun, Zabbar, Paola, Marsa and St Julian's. Every other city and town has less than 10,000 inhabitants, including Gozo's capital and largest city, Victoria (7,000), and the islands' former capital, Mdina (barely 1,000).

The continental lands nearest to the Maltese Islands are Sicily, 58 miles, and Tunisia, 180 miles. The Straits of Gibraltar to the west and the Suez Canal to the east are each about 1,000 miles distant. The archipelago's total land area is 122 square miles, of which the main island occupies 95 square miles, the whole approximating to the Isle of Wight. Between its furthest extremities, Malta itself is 17 miles long from south-east to north-west and 9 miles wide, the equivalent measurements for Gozo being 9 miles and $4\frac{1}{2}$ miles.

Visitors to the islands arriving by air enter through Luqa airport, while the passenger ships calling regularly from Italy and Libya berth in Grand Harbour. Anyone continuing to Gozo or Comino must proceed by the traditional ferry from Marfa, at the north end of the main island, or by hydrofoil from Valletta; these services are infrequent and may be suspended in stormy weather. Buses from Valletta connect with the ferry departures from Marfa, and buses to Victoria await the ferry's arrivals in Gozo. This inter-capital journey by bus-ferry-bus, over a distance of twenty miles, takes about two and a half hours. For anyone not in a hurry it offers various fine examples of Maltese towns, countryside and coastline, an entertaining voyage over the water, and the chance to meet all sorts of Maltese people going about their daily business.

GETTING AROUND

Apart from the maritime links between Malta, Comino and Gozo, internal transport in the Maltese Islands is entirely by road.

Page 17: Valletta, Sliema and the coast towards Gozo: a modern view.

Page 18: Valletta and Grand Harbour from seaward: about 1750.

The former network of ferries serving Valletta and the communities bordering Grand and Marsamxett Harbours has been discontinued, and it is many years since the Maltese could experience travel by train or tram. Public transport is provided today by a large assortment of gaily-painted single-deck buses. In Malta, most routes fan out from two termini on the Valletta-Floriana boundary; in Gozo there is a similar though more modest pattern, with Victoria as its focal point.

While the Maltese road system for the most part might more aptly be termed a winding country lane system, modern improvements are fast making their mark at some of the places where traffic is densest. Road surfaces are generally good but sign-posting is sparse and, to the stranger, confusing. In most cities and towns the narrow streets, many without pavements, are quite unsuitable for the growing volume of traffic; and, with by-passing on the required scale out of the question, the present onslaught of vehicles poses a serious threat to urban life and pedestrian peace of mind.

The main island is an oval plateau sloping gently towards the south-east, tilted eastward from the west-coast cliffs, the highest point being no more than 800 feet above sea level. Its outline is scarred here and there by bays and inlets, not least by the deeply-indented harbours surrounding Valletta which, throughout history, have been the islands' most coveted asset. To the northward the land undulates and the visitor, making his way along the valleys and over the hills, gains an impression of space and distance; a mainland rather than an island quality. This impression is enhanced by the tranquil and timeless character of the countryside, with its terraced fields and rocky escarpments; its medieval villages with their splendid twin-towered churches; the meandering country roads and the leisurely, good-humoured demeanor of the country folk.

The geological structure of the islands is a series of sandwiches of soft globigerina limestone, with fillings of green sand and blue

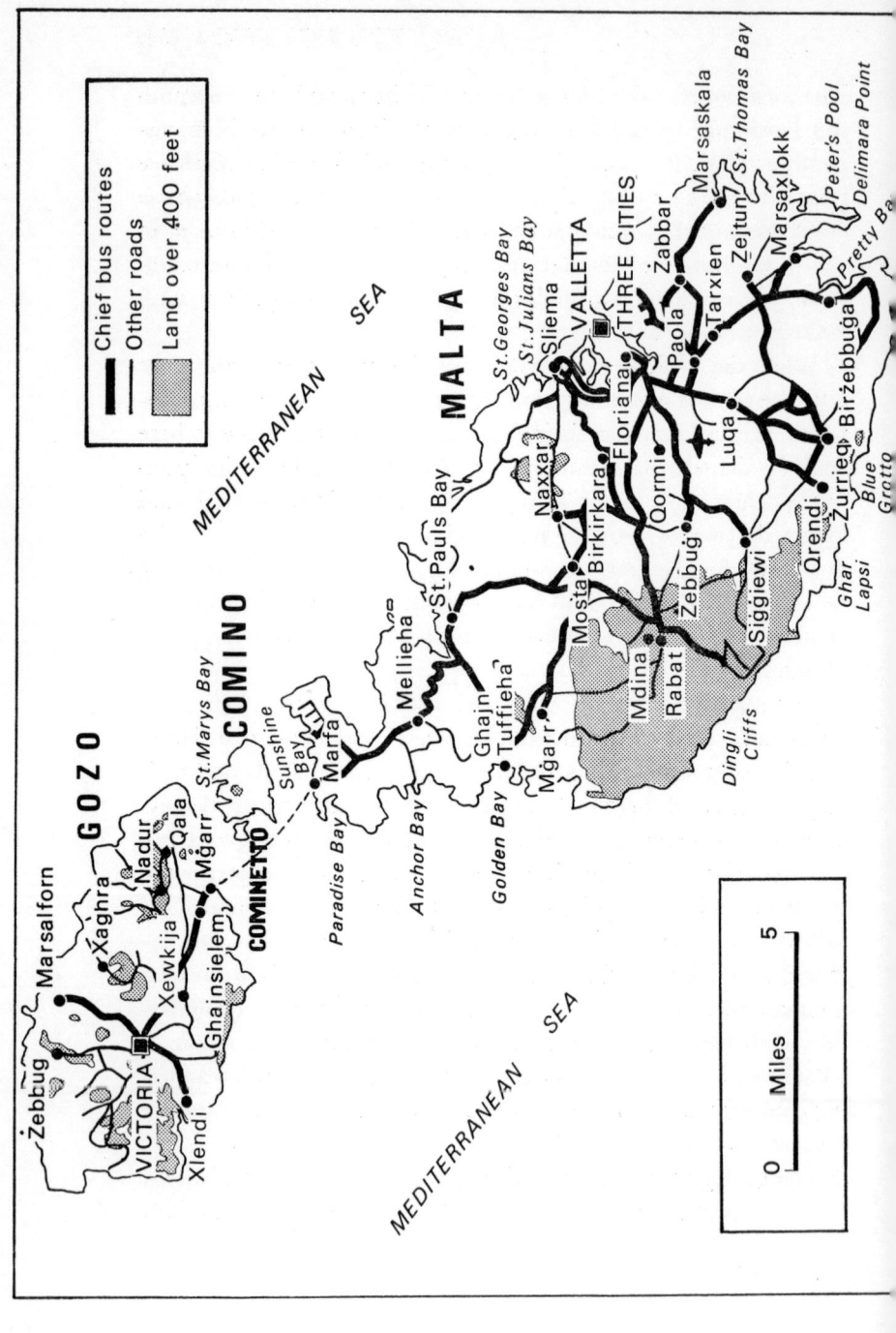

clay between harder crusts of corralline limestone. Apart from the verdant and cultivated areas, the uniform colour of the landscape, including the cities and the rural habitations, is derived from the abundant limestone, an easily worked and aesthetically satisfying building material; another Maltese asset.

A further asset is the healthy climate. The islands experience hot dry summers and mild moist winters; the rainfall, which averages 20 inches a year, occurs mainly from November to February. Strong winds and storms of short duration are liable occasionally to interrupt the spring and late autumn sunshine. The summer months are virtually rainless, the heat being tempered by sea breezes. Average temperatures vary between about 54F in January and 79F in July. In winter the average daily sunshine is 6 hours and in summer $10\frac{1}{2}$ hours. In spring and autumn the visitor will need clothes suitable for an English summer, with slightly warmer clothing in winter and the lightest possible apparel in summer.

WAY OF LIFE

Since 1964, the Maltese nation has been an independent country within the Commonwealth. It is governed by a house of representatives with fifty members elected on a basis of proportional representation from ten electoral divisions. The Queen, represented by a governor general, is the head of parliament, and cabinet ministers are appointed by the governor general on the prime minister's advice.

The constitution is liberal, embodying safeguards for the liberty of the individual in line with British tradition. The judiciary, whose members include six judges and nine magistrates, are independent of the executive in the discharge of their duties. There is compulsory education for all children between six and fourteen years of age with opportunities for further education at the island's university and technical colleges. There are enlightened social and health services. The Roman catholic apostolic religion

21

is by law the religion of the country but liberty of conscience and freedom to worship are an established facet of the constitution.

The life and development of the Maltese people has for many centuries been conditioned by two influences: conquest and religious faith. Due to the islands' strategic position, few of the dominant Mediterranean powers throughout recorded history have been able to resist the temptation to acquire, occupy and rule an archipelago which, but for geographical accident, might well have been bypassed by history.

Of all the implanted cultures which have left their mark on the Maltese Islands, those of the Knights (from 1530 to 1798) and of the British (since 1800) have been pre-eminent. The continuing thread of influence, however, which in strength has always rivalled that of the ruling powers, has been the Church and since the year 60, when St Paul landed inadvertently in Malta, religion has been the consolation and inspiration of the Maltese people. If the power of the church is today suffering a gradual process of erosion it remains nevertheless a most potent factor in the islanders' life.

A less conspicuous and, latterly, a diminishing force in Maltese life has been the nobility. The older families, substantial land-owners over many centuries, living in quiet splendour in their Mdina homes, amassed large fortunes, much of which was invested abroad beyond the grasp of both invader and local politician; these families are still, potentially, a rich source of capital for new enterprises in the islands.

Externally, the noble families have in the past identified themselves most closely with Italy. Internally, with awkward pride, they have tended to remain aloof from the occupying powers, being more concerned with their own affairs than with the political round in Valletta. Today their numbers are dwindling due to emigration, lack of new blood and failure to adapt to social change. Yet they are less on the defensive than they were and, in a busy country whose small size and large families make for tolerance and dynamism in human relations, there is new scope for their energies and talents.

Besides the church, the focal points of ordinary Maltese life have long been the family and the town or village it inhabits. Parochial ties and attitudes are very marked. The citizen of Valletta regards Gozo as a provincial backwater and seldom goes out of his way to visit it. The Gozitan looks with suspicion on his cousins on the 'mainland', ever watchful that his own island will get its fair share of perks and benefits.

NEW TRENDS

The most popular sport is association football. Dancing and cinema-going are long-established recreations. As motoring spreads, swimming, aquatic sports and family picnics gain favour. The Maltese love of an occasional flutter is satisfied partly by the national lottery and, for the better-off, by the fine new casino. There are many small indoor bars and few pavement cafés; apart from the evening stroll in the market place, conviviality is largely out of sight.

Until recently, so were the women. Emancipation came slowly but is gathering speed. Children are adored and pampered and their welfare comes first, but wives and mothers need no longer feel tied by custom to the home. The demurely dimpled maiden of yesterday has evolved quite suddenly into today's slim and self-reliant young woman, enjoying new freedoms in learning, work and play.

A newcomer to the Maltese scene is the tourist, now an important source of prosperity for the islanders. Their country is also proving attractive to investors, industrialists, traders, writers and settlers. The government offers significant inducements to suitable businessmen and immigrants : finance, factories and tax holidays for the former; lenient rates of personal taxation and a low cost of living for the latter. Those seeking to benefit have to meet fairly stringent criteria. The businessman's intentions must be in line with official economic policy and show promise of success, while the settler must bring enough capital or income to ensure self-support. The Maltese can ill afford to carry passengers for their islands are at a difficult stage of transition. Independence is a spur to achievement but the obstacles in the way of economic viability are substantial. Salvation depended formerly upon God and the resident garrison; today's governors, it seems, are productivity, balance of trade and the popular vote.

Fortunately the islands possess assets more precious than harbours, rock and climate, and these are the wit, grit and resilience of the people. The visitor to this archipelago, aware of its long history of endurance and adaptation, conscious of the stalwart and persistent character of its people, will feel not only that the Maltese deserve their success but that they are moving surely and steadily towards its attainment.

2   *THE COVETED ISLANDS*

THE strategic position of the Maltese Islands astride the
sea lanes of the central Mediterranean, coupled with the
main island's superb natural harbours and a terrain
favouring the defender, have long made these islands a coveted
possession and, during much of their history, a pawn in Mediterranean power politics. The earliest settlers are believed to have
crossed from Sicily six thousand years ago to establish a small
farming community. Remains of temples, habitations, tools and
pottery indicate that these and others who followed later
achieved a continuity of existence throughout the next thirty
centuries.

Maltese recorded history dates from about 800 BC, at which
time the Phoenicians were the most influential people in the
area; Malta certainly became a trading post on their copper
route from Palestine to Cornwall. A Phoenician colony took root
and it is mainly to this group that the present-day Maltese prefer
to owe their origins. While it is debatable how much the people
and their tongue can truly claim to be Phoenician, Malta undoubtedly has the distinction of representing one of the last
remaining pockets of the Punic empire.

By the seventh century BC, the Greeks had emerged as a rival
Mediterranean force. Greek coins and pots found on Malta
suggest there might have been a settlement, but it seems more
likely that the Greeks traded without settling; joint inscriptions in
Greek and Phoenician indicate that Malta, for once, managed
to hold a balanced position between two rival powers.

The sixth century BC was a high point in Malta's internal
development. An inscription shows that it had a democratic
government with a senate and an assembly of the people, similar

to that of a Greek city state. The Greek historian, Diodorus, noted :

> Malta is furnished with many and very good harbours, and the inhabitants are very rich, for it is full of all sorts of artificers among whom there are excellent weavers of fine linen. Their houses are very stately and beautiful, adorned with graceful eaves and pargetted with white plaster.

ROMAN OCCUPATION

The shift of Mediterranean power to Rome, and the ensuing clash between the Republic and Carthage, focused attention on Malta's strategic importance. The islands possibly changed hands several times between the two. Livy mentions the visit of a consul to Malta in 216 BC, but it is not known whether this marked the beginning of Roman rule or was merely a reconnaissance.

By 146 BC, however, the Romans, having sacked Carthage, were definitely established on Malta, which was eventually made a municipality with the right to create laws, administer justice and issue currency. Overall control of the islands was vested in a governor and there is no doubt that Malta suffered from the system that allowed unscrupulous officials to treat annexed territories as money boxes to be raided and emptied at will. Verres, who came under fire from Cicero's powerful rhetoric in 70 BC, was probably the rule rather than the exception; during his time as governor he never once visited the islands, but they were obliged to send him the very best of their honey, cloth and women's garments.

Malta appears to have remained a prosperous trading station throughout Roman rule. The Temple of Juno, on the site of Fort St Angelo, became a famous shrine, but the Maltese themselves treasure an accident in AD 60 as the most important event of the period. St Paul, travelling to Rome to appeal against a charge of heresy, was shipwrecked on the north coast of the main island.

Stranded for three months, he set the cornerstone of a faith that wound itself deep into the soul of the people and ever afterwards provided the one solid base in their otherwise insecure lives.

For nearly five hundred years after the end of Roman rule, Malta's history is largely conjecture. When Theodosius divided the empire between his two sons in 395, the islands were included in the eastern half. Gothic coins found on the island suggest a Vandal occupation at some stage, while coins and evidence of a garrison seem to prove that Malta came under Byzantine sway.

THE ARABS TAKE OVER

The Arabs were the next people to come to prominence in the Mediterranean and in a hundred years they built up an empire almost as large as that of the Romans. Once established in Sicily, they naturally made forays into nearby Malta and, in 870, conquered the islands. Under Islamic rule only members of the Islamic faith could be free men; the rest were slaves. That many Maltese found it expedient to change religion is understandable; that a healthy nucleus of Christians remained is a tribute both to the strength of the islanders' faith and to the tolerance of their rulers. It seems likely that the Arabs treated Christianity rather as present-day Russians do—as an unofficial fact. The Bishop of Malta was left in office for eight years and landed in jail only when caught sending wheat to Christians besieged in Syracuse by the Arabs. A census taken in 991 showed 3,500 Christians to 13,000 Muslims on Malta, but twice as many Christians as Muslims on Gozo.

Because of internal wars in the Arabic empire, the islands were often left much to themselves and the Maltese appear to have had their own local assembly and fleet. In 1049 their situation improved even further when Christians were offered their freedom in return for repulsing a Byzantine attack; a chronicler of the time reported a preponderance of Christians throughout the islands.

At the same period a Norman, Tancred de Hautville, was busy creating a principality for himself in southern Italy after passing through on his way back from a pilgrimage to the Holy Land. His son, Count Roger, planned to make Sicily more secure by conquering Malta. In 1090 he made a mock attack on St Paul's Bay to draw the Arab forces, while behind their backs he scaled the western cliffs and took the garrison by surprise. At first, as part of the Kingdom of Sicily, Malta fared well. Roger was an enlightened conqueror who levied moderate taxes and allowed his possessions virtually to govern themselves. Maltese Muslims appear to have been left in peace; one gold coin of the period shows King Roger on one side and on the other the inscription 'There is only one God and Mahammed is the prophet of God.'

The history of the three confused centuries after Roger is neatly summed up in Allister Macmillan's book *Malta and Gibralter* as 'an alternation of grants and repeals of feudal rights, of abuse of power and conferment of privileges—in fine, a mere recital of the ups and downs that marked the evolution of feudalism on the continent.'

A SUCCESSION OF RULERS

During the crusades Malta was an important link in the Christians' lines of defence against the Muslims, although Muslims in fact lived peaceably on the island until persecuted and finally harried out by Frederick II of Aragon in the middle of the thirteenth century. Rule of the islands passed from the Normans to the Suabians and on to the Angevins by inheritance and then to the Spanish by conquest. Whatever the nationality of the ruler, he tended to regard Malta as an inanimate piece of property to be pawned or disposed of at will. In the early thirteenth century it was virtually a perquisite of the Grand Admiral of Sicily; in 1320 King Alphonso, needing some ready cash, mortgaged the island to two noblemen in turn. The Maltese were so miserable that they paid off the second of these with 30,000 florins in order to go back under the Spanish crown.

While masters, royal or otherwise, were exercising their absentee prerogative and raiding the islands' meagre resources, Malta was being harassed from the sea by pirates. Berbers, Turks, even at one stage fellow Christians, brought terror to the poorly defended islands. In one classic raid, long commemorated in Maltese folk lore, Barbary corsairs carried off four hundred inhabitants, including a complete wedding party. Malta, for its part, was probably not slow to set up a pirate fleet.

In the early sixteenth century, as the economy continued to swing between prosperity and famine, powers in other lands were setting the stage for the most glorious period of Maltese history. The Knights of the Order of St John of Jerusalem were soon to make their home on the islands. The Knights at this time—devout, aristocratic, warlike—formed one of the most powerful groups in Europe. They owned large tracts of land in several countries, were reputed to be almost as rich as the church itself, and boasted the bluest of blood among their members. But they had one major problem—they lacked a permanent headquarters of their own.

The Order had begun in the eleventh century in a simple hostel on the pilgrim route through Muslim-dominated Palestine into Jerusalem. From tending the poor and sick, the monks developed an efficient security service, providing armed escorts through the dangerous parts of Syria. After the successful First Crusade they had become a military order, confirmed by the Pope in 1113. Christian kings gratefully donated land and money, young aristocrats proudly joined up and when they died their wealth reverted automatically to the Knights. As the Order grew it was divided into eight branches, or *langues*, according to the original nationalities of the members—Aragon, Auvergne, Castille (including Portugal), England, France, Germany, Italy and Provence.

When the kings of Jerusalem were forced to retreat from the Holy Land, the Order withdrew with them. After a long war the Knights won the island of Rhodes; from here they were able to knock hard at the Turkish infidel, enhance their reputation as defenders of the Christian faith, and become recognised as a bulwark to keep Europe safe. But the Turks were eventually provoked into launching a massive assault on Rhodes and in 1522, 90,000 of the Sultan's forces joined battle with 7,000 Knights and Rhodians. The island held out for six months, but superior force prevailed in the end. The sultan spared the Knights, allowing them to quit Rhodes with honour, a leniency which later he had cause to regret.

KNIGHTS IN SEARCH OF A HOME

The Knights went as a matter of course to the Pope, their supreme master. Clement VII, himself a member of the Order, gave its grand master a warm but hesitant welcome. Any hasty move might have offended one or other of the powerful monarchs, Francis I of France and Charles I of Spain. Charles I, seeing a good opportunity to establish another front against the Turks, suggested in 1523 that the Knights might take over the defence of Malta and Tripoli. Malta, a less attractive island than Rhodes, was at least a self-contained, defendable unit; but to hold Tripoli as well at that time would have meant stretching their small forces beyond their capacity. Moreover, Charles expected them to support him in any future Mediterranean war. This could have meant fighting France, and the Order's rules forbade members going to war against a Christian state. Besides, the French *langue* could hardly be expected to do battle with its mother country.

For the next six years the Order remained on tenterhooks while the European balance of power seesawed. Finally the two monarchs became friendly enough with each other and with the Pope for the Knights to feel safe in accepting Malta. Not that

they viewed the prospect with much relish. Their first report had
been gloomy.

> The island of Malta is merely a rock of soft sandstone, about
> six or seven leagues long and three or four broad. The surface of
> the rock is barely covered with three or four feet of earth, which
> is likewise stony, and very unfit to grow corn and other grain . . .
> except for a few springs in the middle of the island there is no
> running water, nor even wells.

But by now the Knights were desperate for a home. The
material conditions were simple : the Order was to give the King
of Spain a falcon a year. Politically, the agreement was to prove
more complicated. The Bishop of Malta was to be chosen from
three nominees by the King of Sicily, who was to hold sovereignty
over the islands, while Maltese rights and privileges were to be
preserved. This last clause must have caused hollow laughter on
the island; when King Alphonso had taken Malta under his wing
he had granted a new charter which promised that the islands
would never again be bartered without the inhabitants' consent.
But no-one bothered to consult the Maltese in this latest trans-
action and they were hardly in a position to start a fight with
Christianity's toughest soldiers.

In November 1530 Fra Philippe Villiers de l'Isle Adam, Grand
Master of the Knights, entered Mdina, the capital of Malta. The
Knights, venerated by rich and poor throughout Europe, were
sensible of their power and glory. Behind the grand façade, however, they were not entirely supermen. Of their three vows—
poverty, chastity, obedience—the first was by now redundant, the
second in abeyance and the third somewhat dented by the younger
members. But their reputation for valour was soon to be upheld.
Christian Europe was generally in a weak state and in the next
thirty years suffered repeated setbacks from the Turks, who ended
up dominating most of the Mediterranean. Malta was a constant
source of irritation to them and the Knights were perpetually
threatened. In 1565, hearing of a massive build-up of troops in

Constantinople, the Order sent out urgent appeals to Christian rulers for help in what they sensed would shortly become a do-or-die combat; at this time, Grand Master de Valette had only eight war galleys and 9,000 men at his command.

The siege at Rhodes had taught the Knights to leave the countryside bare of people, animals and crops, and to turn the fortifiable points into war cities, fully stocked with food, water and ammunition. As the inland capital of Mdina seemed vulnerable, Malta's defence rested ultimately on the Grand Harbour complex, particularly St Elmo fort at the seaward end of Mount Sceberras (now Valletta), St Angelo fort at the tip of Birgu (now Vittoriosa), and St Michael's fort on the Senglea promontory.

As the sun rose on 18 May, the horizon filled with white sails emblazoned with the Sultan's red crescent, and the Great Siege of Malta began. The 38,000 invaders were confident that they would soon subjugate the small band of islanders. But four elements were to help the Order: clever tactics, heroism, luck and a brilliant leader. De Valette was tough, brave and single-minded; when the odds seemed hopeless, he imbued his men with religious fervour and a real sense of destiny. On the other hand, the Turkish command was virtually split between three leaders, the cause of several fatal mistakes.

The naval commander, obsessed by the need to gain an anchorage for his fleet, persuaded his colleagues to concentrate their opening assault on St Elmo, manned by 100 knights and 500 soldiers. These de Valette ordered to fight to the last, knowing that the Sicilian monarch had promised to help on condition that the Knights still held the fort. Its garrison, aware that the length of their survival would determine the outcome of the whole campaign, hung on as men died and walls collapsed under day and night bombardment. Besieged from the sea and from the high ground of Sceberras, they could not expect to hold out indefinitely. The Turks had estimated three days; they finally occupied it, massacring the last few defenders, in five weeks. Replacements crossed the Grand Harbour to the fortress up to the last week, knowing that the outcome of their bravery was almost certain death. But the sacrifice made all the difference, giving the Knights time to consolidate the defences of the other forts.

Never was Malta's unique position more important. All Europe realised what was at stake. As Queen Elizabeth of England said, 'If the Turks should prevail against the Isle of Malta, it is uncertain what further peril might follow to the rest of Christendom.' Italy, France and Spain would be open to Turkish invasion. Several countries joined in anxious prayer.

The advance force from Sicily arrived despite the fate of St Elmo. It numbered only 600 men but, achieving surprise, it made a vital difference. The Knights, their luck holding, were warned by a Turkish deserter about a plan for Senglea to be attacked from the south, and this gave the Order time to build a line of defensive stakes which succesfully repulsed the attack.

The defenders were now ringed by Turks, with St Michael's fort, the weaker of the two survivors, crumbling daily under the massive onslaught of guns and men. Yet again fate came to the aid of the Knights. One thousand Turks, sailing across the harbour, fell into a well-prepared trap: hidden guns caught them broadside on and destroyed them. Then, at a crucial point in the battle, a Turkish post in the rear was caught unawares by a band of Christians. Word spread through the Turkish forces that a large army from Sicily was about to attack and the commander, believing himself outnumbered, sounded the retreat. But the supposed van of the Christian battalions was found to be merely a local force from Mdina that had come along to see if it could help.

The Turks then tried to take Senglea with the aid of two huge towers, built like scaffolds, by which troops could scale the walls.

But the Knights demolished one by shooting unexpectedly through openings at the base of the walls, and the other by a hand-to-hand attack through the same openings. Just as de Valette had exhorted St Elmo to fight to the end, so now he wrought every ounce of courage out of the besieged in St Michael's. During the toughest phase, he crossed from his headquarters in St Angelo to join in the battle himself—he was seventy-one.

THE TIDE TURNS

The untenable was held and, as de Valette had planned, the Turks were forced to divide their fire between the two forts. Under continuous bombardment, few of the defenders remained uninjured. Their heroism reached the sublime. Anyone able to walk was considered able to work. The Knights fought in high summer temperatures in full armour, with leather or quilted jerkins underneath; not surprisingly, a few of them died from heat stroke. Requests for assistance were smuggled repeatedly out of the island. The Maltese were one with the Knights, determined, whatever the cost, to be rid of the Turkish invader—though of the nobles there is barely a word in contemporary records; presumably they sat it out in their palaces in Mdina.

The Turks were now weary and despondent, with nearly a third of their forces killed, large numbers struck by disease and food and ammunition in short supply. The quick blow had passed through slow strangulation to stalemate, with the aggressor's suffering no less than his victim's.

The nervous Turks were tricked once more when the main relief force set out at last from Syracuse with 8,000 Spanish and Italian soldiers. A storm prevented half of them from landing but the Muslim commanders, unaware of this setback, hastily embarked their troops. Learning the truth, they made one more assault on Malta but the fresh opposing forces were too much for their dispirited men and on 8 September, the feast of the Birth of

Page 35: (above) Harbour ceremony: Admiral's Salute: about 1930; (below) Harbour ceremony: *Ohio's* arrival, 1942.

Page 36 : Bomb damage in Valletta, 1942.

the Virgin, the Turks sailed home with only a quarter of their army intact, leaving Malta to its tattered peace.

Malta had lost 219 Knights and over 9,000 inhabitants. Fortifications, villages, farms, crops were in ruins. But de Valette's genius quickly rekindled the islanders' spirit with a massive peacetime project; the building of a fortified city on Sceberras, the lofty spit of land between the two main harbours. This he called Valletta.

Ironically, as Malta became more impregnable, it began to lose much of its strategic value. The battle of Lepanto in 1571 dealt a decisive blow to Turkish sea power and, although Mediterranean skirmishes recurred during the next 150 years, Islam no longer constituted a serious threat. Europe's energies were directed westward towards the newly-discovered lands across the Atlantic. And if Malta was called into battle again, the Knights' long rowing galleys could be no match for the large new sailing ships.

The Order, declining into a flabby and dissolute middle-age, elected elderly men to the office of grand master, their early death ensuring a high turnover for the coveted post; its leaders quarrelled with the Pope, the local citizenry and among themselves. The Maltese people were kept in a state of poverty, their rights gradually whittled away, their grain supply dependent on the whims or the nationality of the reigning grand master; supplies from Sicily rose when he was Spanish, and fell when he was French. Despotic grand masters squeezed every penny they could out of the population; many of the wilier Maltese escaped poverty the only way they could, by joining the already swollen ranks of privileged clergy.

When royal and aristocratic rule ended in France in 1792, shock waves began to hit the Order. Its French possessions were seized and in other countries there began an erosion into the Knights' wealth; in Germany, Spain, Portugal, Sicily and Naples, the Order was either taken over or heavily taxed. Income fell from 3 million livres in 1788 to 1 million in 1797, and the grand master had to sell jewels and melt down plate in compensation. As revolutionary ideas filtered through to the islands, the mixture of arrogant masters and impoverished peasants made a fertile breeding ground for discontent.

A CHANCE FOR FRANCE

At this point Napoleon, sensing a new strategic role for Malta which he saw as the key to his planned undermining of Britain's Indian Empire, swung into action. By 1798 he could call on enough Republican support on the islands to take them with scarcely a fight. The Knights and their grand master, pensioned off, sailed ignominiously away within three days of the French conquest.

In a rare miscalculation, Nelson had not realised Malta's importance until it was too late; Napoleon reached the islands just one day ahead of the English squadron. But events were soon to play into England's hands. The Maltese had received the French as liberators, not as despots, and certainly not as desecrators of the faith. The people watched in silent amazement as the occupiers plundered paintings, plate, tapestries and jewellery from the Knights' quarters; they stood by helplessly as their own small savings were stolen and their pensions suspended; but when the French switched their attention to the churches, anger turned swiftly into deeds.

In Mdina the church of Our Lady of Mount Carmel was being ransacked when the inhabitants rose violently against the commandant; local villagers marched into the city to help and the assembled Maltese massacred the entire French detachment. In Valletta the French commander reported that the people resembled 'enraged lions'; besieged by superior numbers, his garrison was forced to retreat inside the walls. The fortress, built to keep the enemy out, now served to keep him in.

It was one thing to rise against a small garrison, another to fight Napoleon himself. The Maltese set up their own temporary government, and declared themselves subjects of the King of Naples. But, the king being in far too weak a position to be of much help, there seemed to be only one suitable power which might finish the job of ousting the French—Great Britain.

Nelson, having met two Maltese envoys on his way back from the Battle of the Nile, immediately asked his Portuguese allies to start a blockade. British ships joined in, among them one commanded by Captain (later Sir) Alexander Ball. This sensitive, intelligent man, put ashore in Malta as Britain's representative, emerged as the islands' leader during the blockade and held office as the envoy of the King of Naples.

The French garrison held out for two years and two days, during which time both they and the islanders came to the verge of starvation. In July 1800 1,300 fresh British troops succeeded in taking Valletta, but victory was marred when their commander, new to the island, overrode local opinion and allowed the French to leave with their spoils intact.

The Maltese were by now quite sure how they wanted to be governed—as part of the British Empire—but the European powers could not allow such a strategic stronghold to settle its affairs as simply as that. The Czar of Russia, having strengthened his position by claiming grand mastership of the absent Order, joined England and Naples in an agreement to hold the island in trust for the Knights. When peace was signed at Amiens in 1802, the powers reached a compromise; the Knights were to return to Malta but the grand master would be appointed by the Pope.

The Maltese rioted on receiving this news and a deputation hastened to London to ask George III for his protection. To back up their appeal for admission to the British Empire, they pointed out that 'Malta is not to be taken out of the hands of the English for the purpose of not remaining long in the hands of the Order of

39

St John.' In other words, Malta might as well be handed back direct to France.

Malta became the principal bone of contention between France and England during their uneasy truce. The treaty had promised increased democratic rights for the Maltese, and England claimed she could not leave until certain that these would be realised. In turn, Napoleon claimed that England's extended occupation was a breach of the treaty. 'I would rather put you in possession of the heights of Montmartre than of Malta,' he rashly told the British Ambassador in Paris. Meanwhile, the Order quietly wooed the Maltese by promising cheaper bread. The dance of verbal power ended abruptly at the Battle of Waterloo in 1815 when Britain's defeat of Napoleon confirmed her supremacy in the Mediterranean—and her hold on Malta.

BRITISH COLONY

It was a strange marriage that now took place : Malta, with its strong religion tending towards mysticism after long years of suffering, naïvely pleased at the arrival of what it took to be a just and tolerant master; England, in full imperial power, touched by Malta's overtures rather as a nobleman might be by the gratitude of a new tenant who is then told haughtily to go back to his quarters and get on with the work. G. Percy Badger said: 'The truth is that without the protection of a great maritime power, Malta must be constantly exposed to aggressions.' Cumberland Clark says: 'The ever-present problem is to reconcile the constitutional rights of the Maltese population with the position of Malta as the chief naval base of Britain in the Mediterranean.' The first statement was made in 1879, the second in 1939, and they represent the dilemma of both sides throughout British rule.

With the opening of the Suez Canal in 1869, commercial and strategic interest swung back to the Mediterranean and Malta became one of the vital links in the chain from England to India. The chain was strengthened further when Britain won Cyprus after helping Turkey to fight Russia in 1877. Britain's naval policy was simply to maintain a fleet twice the size of the combination of the next two largest fleets, and Malta justified itself as the key Mediterranean base.

The Mediterranean was hardly secured, however, when a naval threat began to build up nearer England. In the North Sea, a united Germany was flexing its newly-found muscles. Britain transferred her Atlantic fleet to home shores, and the six Mediterranean battleships moved from Malta to Gibraltar whence they could cover either the Mediterranean or the western approaches to England. The Maltese were reminded once again of their lopsided economy as work disappeared from their dockyards.

In 1914, when feints between Germany and England erupted into war, Malta appeared to be trapped. Two powerful German warships were at large in the Mediterranean, Turkey came in on the German side and Italy, by then ruling Tripoli, was a signatory to the Austria-Germany pact. Gradually the threat receded. The warships were penned inside the Dardanelles, and Italy, fearing Austria more than England, decided to join the Allies. During the Gallipoli campaign, Malta became a refuge for the wounded, providing twenty-seven hospitals with 25,000 beds. The dockyard was at full stretch repairing Allied warships damaged in action. Maltese crews manned the Mediterranean minesweeping flotillas. The islands were used also as a prisoner-of-war base.

In the uneasy years of peace after 1918, Malta earned its keep as the headquarters and maintenance base of Britain's most powerful overseas fleet. The confident presence of British naval might in the Mediterranean was strategically both a stabilising factor and an irritant. As Europe began to re-form itself into hostile camps, fascism took hold in Italy. The angry cries of *mare nostrum* and the Italian aggression against Abyssinia were ominous ripples from larger waves building up beyond the horizon.

In Malta, allegiances became strained as Italian-speaking elements struggled to keep their influence. Despite Malta's traditional ties with Italy, however, the islands were still very much part of the Empire, and the Maltese people were soon to prove themselves heroic defenders of freedom in the second European conflict.

3   *INSIDE STORY*

THE Maltese people, under successive rulers, experienced self-government in varying degree. A major step forward was the constitution granted early in the fifteenth century by the King of Sicily, whereby heads of families in every town and village elected representatives from the nobles, intelligentsia, priests and merchants. These formed the *universita*, or *consiglio popolare*. It had no legislative authority but, besides advising the king on Maltese needs, it had the power to organise the food supply and collect taxes.

Later, under the Knights, official posts were still filled by Maltese, appointed by the grand master. The *universita* gradually lost its powers until by the eighteenth century it had little to do except manipulate the grain supply. A capital sum, paying depositors 5 per cent, was used to buy grain from Sicily and the officials, called *jurats*, fixed the selling price to yield their organisation a small profit; an intelligent system that protected the Maltese against famine or speculators.

As the Order's influence in Europe waned, so their despotic rule over the islands hardened. The eighteenth century Grand Master, Rohan, formulated a new code of laws calling on the advice of a Neapolitan lawyer who believed that torture was civilisation's safeguard. The code was correspondingly harsh, thirteen crimes carrying the death penalty. The Maltese, with an almost oriental resignation, retreated more and more into the consolation of their religion; the nobles, deprived of power or influence, took refuge in their own self-contained world, earning just enough from their estates to keep going, but seldom enough to expand their activities.

NAPOLEONIC UPHEAVAL

The first impact of modern ideas on these feudal islands was cataclysmic. Napoleon was in Malta for only seven days but in that time he turned the islands upside down. Nobility was abolished, all Maltese being declared equal in rights. Fifteen elementary schools were started, to teach French, the French constitution and French morality. Marriage was to be a civil ceremony. The number of ecclesiastics was severely limited and no religious order was allowed more than one convent. The Pope's power over church affairs was abolished. The number of judges was cut from eight to one.

When the British arrived in 1800 to help oust the iconoclastic French, they had no ideological interest in the islands, which were regarded purely as a military base. As a matter of form they declared that the crown of England would protect 'your churches, your holy religion, your persons, your property' but in truth, the British, having seen the dissolution of France throw the whole of Europe into war, were nervous of radical changes in the established order. Their colonies were part of a huge trade network that was to make England the richest country in the world; if rapacity seemed too base a motive for building up an empire, they could always plead the protection of the world's most civilised nation.

Between 1803 and 1813 neither side had much time to appreciate the import of their union, for England was too busy with the war and the Maltese were too busy making money. The British civil commissioners ruled 'with the tacit consent of the people' but the reforms they carried out were insignificant. The first Commissioner, Alexander Ball, was faced with a disintegrated civil service; letters and documents were in complete disarray, some staff had left with the French and, in the end, it took ten years to sort out the public accounts. He increased the number of judges to a more practical three and passed a few Acts relating to such minor matters as vagabondage, damage to fortifications, and the roaming of pigs through Valletta.

It was fortuitous that the first commissioner should be one who cared genuinely for the Maltese people, and they for him. Restricted on the large level, his philanthropy found outlets on the small. A military doctor described one of his horticultural plans:

> He rendered a barren surface near each village, often a naked rock, fit for cultivation . . . he enclosed it with a high wall, provided it with young trees, shrubs and plants and gave this, as an additional income, to the justice of peace of each village; obliging him, at the same time, to give gratis to each petitioner of his village seeds of his plants, to share his shrubbery and to allow the people to graft from his trees.

BRITAIN TAKES STOCK

Such halcyon co-operation was not to last; with the Napoleonic wars out of the way, the two countries could begin to take stock of one another. England was to learn that Malta, no longer propped up with Knightly money, was not quite the sturdy protégé it had seemed; and the Maltese were to discover that England was not quite the kindly patron they had expected. England's principal European possession seemed to be just as backward as some of the Empire's remoter communities. General education was almost nil, a largely illiterate population relying on clergy and gentry for knowledge and information. Land had remained in the same hands for nearly 500 years, one-third owned by the church, one-third by the occupying government, and one-third by private landlords who had subjected much of it to perpetual entail.

The legal system had become less a protection of rights than a source of income for lawyers. An 1813 visitor, Blaquiere, observed:

> Justice has ceased to be little more than an empty sound, and the people have nearly forgotten that they were once governed by

laws which secured property, punished crimes, and promoted that degree of confidence so necessary to the well being of a state.

There was no proper law training. 'Thus', said Blaquiere, 'you daily see persons of the most ignorant description engage in the law, where it would seem that chicanery and fraud are sufficient to supply the want of honesty and talent.' Cases could be prolonged indefinitely by the mass of legal devices so that eventually the richest man won; neither plaintiff nor defendant could be called as a witness; hearsay evidence was accepted and police warrants did not need magisterial authority.

The British, their sense of fair play outraged, were confused to find that the Maltese actually enjoyed such a complicated system. In 1826 a traveller commented :

> The men in Malta may be said, without much exaggeration, to talk of nothing but law, which in their eyes assumes a greater importance than commerce itself. Many of the Maltese engage in a law-suit purely for the pleasure they experience in carrying it on.

The agricultural system, on the other hand, had been transformed over the centuries into a triumph of man over matter. The Maltese had contrived to turn virtually barren rock into a prolific market garden. Stones broken into small pieces lay about a foot deep on the rock, with a second layer of more finely powdered stones above. Precious earth made two more layers, separated by dung. During the hot rainless summer, dew forming at night was retained by the underlying clay. In this ground, farmers managed an intensive crop-rotation such as melons for two years, cotton in the third and corn in the fourth.

But here too, medievalism had cramped development. Most farms, rented on short leases of four to six years' duration, were too small. Tenants could make a bare living in a good season but would lack the money for expansion. The owners were usually impoverished nobles who lived solely on their farm rents, scorning other sources of income; the expense of operating short leases and collecting the rent from bankrupt farmers left little in reserve for agricultural improvement.

THE BOOM YEARS

At the start of the nineteenth century, when cotton was a primary source of livelihood for the population, involving not only the farmers but hundreds of cottage workers who spun and wove it, Spain, their main buyer, dealt the Maltese a hard blow with its ban on cotton imports. But the islanders, luckily, were on the threshold of a boom—from 1803 to 1813, they prospered as never before.

During this period, Malta was created a free port and, with France and England indulging in a mutual blockade, soon became one of England's chief trading centres. English merchants switched their activities from other Mediterranean countries to Valletta; commercial houses flourished and warehouse space was at a premium. 'The Maltese congratulated themselves on the banishment of want from the land of their birth,' said a contemporary historian, and the civil commissioner painted a utopian view of Malta's future. 'Commerce, being now extended, arts and sciences encouraged, manufactures and agriculture supported, and industry rewarded, Malta will become the Emporium of the Mediterranean and the seat of content.' But this short burst of prosperity was no remedy for a basically unstable financial situation where rates of interest rose as high as 12 per cent, where the people were by nature too wary to invest in their own traders, and where the food markets were run on monopolistic lines.

The nobles were among the first to test their rights against the British Empire; according to the nobility, the Knights had illegally suppressed the *consiglio popolare* in 1782, and the restoration of this ancient body was now demanded. The claim was spoiled by several facts: the *consiglio popolare* had never enjoyed effective legislative powers; by 1782 it had virtually ceased to exist and the

47

nobles themselves had done little over the years to prevent its demise. They persevered. In 1811 they proclaimed that the Maltese were being 'deluded, flattered and misused' by the 'terror, suppression and despotism' of the British administration, and they stepped up their demands with firm requests for a free press and for trial by jury.

Sir Hildebrand Oakes, Commissioner at that time, couched his reply in equally strong terms; the petition, he said, was the work of 'a few turbulent and factious individuals' bent on a 'scandalous libel' who chose to ignore the powerful protection and commercial advantages of the British fleet's presence. As a token gesture, he and two other British officials were formed into a commission to consider the question of a Maltese constitution, but in cool, sonorous tones they were to keep Maltese democracy at bay.

> So firmly are we persuaded of the mischievous effects that would result from entrusting any portion of political power to a people so singularly unfitted to enjoy it, that, with a view to the real happiness of the Maltese we have no hesitation in saying that, were the pretensions to a former existence of a deliberative legislative assembly as clear and incontestable as they really are obscure and groundless, we should still feel it our duty to recommend most earnestly a positive refusal of its re-establishment as a measure fraught with the greatest danger and involving the most ruinous consequences.

In practical terms, the commission recommended that the offices of civil commissioner and military commander should be merged into a governorship, and they suggested that the governor be advised by a council of four British and four Maltese, all to be nominated by himself.

HARD MAN, HARD TIMES

Two events in 1813 were to have a profound effect on the Maltese Islands. A plague epidemic killed a fifth of the population, and Sir Thomas Maitland was made governor. Malta, in the middle of the Mediterranean trading area, was always exposed to disease, but this was its worst ever infection. From the death of a shoe-maker's daughter, the plague spread swiftly. A contemporary writer describes the scene: 'The streets silent and deserted; persons passing each other without salutation, only anxious to avoid contact; no business, no intercourse of friendship . . .' Trade came virtually to a standstill and within three months the government faced bankruptcy. Economic miracle had become economic disaster. A 6 per cent loan was tried but this raised a mere £18,000; after two months, only £20,000 remained in the treasury and England had to lend £130,000.

At this point Sir Thomas Maitland arrived on the scene. He was self-educated and outspoken, a fanatic for work and intolerant of other people's problems and difficulties. Nicknamed King Tom, he brought autocratic rule back to Malta; although he caused a great deal of bitterness, only a man with his strength of will could have broken the island's economic labyrinth to lay the foundations of a viable modern state.

He scorned the commission's suggestion of an advisory council but, to pacify the nobles, he created six regional lord lieutenants. The commission having recommended a new legal system, Maitland had one working within a year.

The great principle upon which it is the intention of His Majesty that the Government of these islands should be conducted is that there should be a complete separation between the Executive, the Legislative and the Judicial Authorities . . .

He itemised the two main abuses :

Firstly, the strong supposition, if not the certainty, that the habit of corrupting the judges, existed; secondly, that the judges themselves to enhance their consequence and to add to their power and influence set all law at naught and decided exactly as suited their immediate ends and purposes.

The judges were to be paid fixed salaries instead of fees, and, to keep verdicts straight, a high court of appeal with, above it, a supreme council of justice, were set up. Although the governor presided over the second, thus breaking the rule of separation between executive and judicial power, Maitland said judges would be less bribable if everyone knew verdicts could be rescinded from the top.

The judges naturally objected to the curtailment of their powers and, when the *universita* came under the axe, there were even more protests. Maitland, in typical language, had called it a 'dung-hill of corruption'; the *jurats* were disorganised, unbusiness-like and probably unscrupulous, the accounts were in a mess and the whole concern was run at a loss. For twelve years, however, bread had been cheaper in Malta than at other leading Mediterranean ports. Maitland, having abolished the organisation, created a government monopoly; this began profitably, but ultimately was no more successful than the *universita*. A few years later the grain trade reverted to private enterprise.

THE CHURCH AT ODDS

With the advent of sweeping reforms the Maltese realised that there would be no return to a subsidised *laissez-faire*; while Britain perceived that, even when the more feudal institutions had been modernised, harmony would be marred by the deep feelings aroused on the questions of religion and language.

> Other than in remote Quebec, the British had not—perhaps never would—encounter a Church medieval, a Church militant, and a Church that had lived under a theocracy long after the era of the national state had modified the feudalism of Europe.

Thus Harrison Smith sums up. It was not just a question of creed. When a protestant lieutenant in the British army objected to firing a gun salute to celebrate a catholic festival, he was court-martialled and dismissed. Britain might control Malta but the Church controlled the people and to achieve success, Britain had to work through the Church. There was a natural antipathy among protestants towards the power of the Church, as witness numerous outbursts in travel books of the time.

> Priests and friars are met at every step, and still retain over the minds of a superstitious people an unbounded and despotic sway . . . poor wretches, they have been and still are, ground and devoured by their clergy. The priests and monks have a fine time of it here.

The Church gave in gracefully when, in 1828, the ecclesiastical courts were restricted to ecclesiastical matters. But the archbishop always had to be deferred to, and had to be seen to be deferred to; in state processions he was placed immediately after the governor and before all other officials. Maitland and the then archbishop were involved in slightly bizarre negotiations after the plague, when a thanksgiving service was held. The archibshop having been used to occupying the grand master's throne, neither he nor Maitland could allow the other to be seen sitting in such state. They finally reached a compromise by sitting on either side of the throne, which was left empty as the 'emblem of His Majesty's Sovereignty in these islands.'

More serious were the entanglements between Church and state on non-ecclesiastical matters. The Church was almost more nervous than were the British of press freedom, fearing it would lead to anti-catholic attacks. Even economics were affected. One of Malta's claims to fame was its staggering density of population and fast-rising birthrate. Whereas in 1525 there had been thirteen inhabitants to the square mile, by 1833 there were 1,110, giving the highest density in the world. With the Church encouraging early marriage and large families, the average number of children per marriage was ten, reduced by infant mortality to five survivors.

Unemployment grew as trade slumped after the boom years, and the British and Maltese reached an impasse. 'Give us work,' cried the Maltese. 'Limit your growing population,' growled the British. The government's attempt to introduce a minimum age limit for marriage was resisted by the Church. The government indulged in subtle propaganda, including the printing of 'health' articles which claimed that a man decayed three years earlier for every year under twenty-one that he married. The Maltese preferred to decay earlier.

THE LANGUAGE ISSUE

The language problem was to bedevil the islands' politics right up to independence. As Maltese had no written format, Italian had gradually become the indigenous written language and, consequently, the spoken language of the literate sections of the community. In 1813 the secretary of state had written to Maitland :

> The attention of His Majesty's Government is turned to the means of effecting a gradual advancement in the condition and information of the People, and of identifying their Affections and Interests with the British Connection. With this view, I recommend to your constant attention the Diffusion of the English Language among the inhabitants; and the promotion of every method by which the English may be brought to supersede the Italian Tongue.

In an Alice in Wonderland way, the British seemed to expect the Maltese to speak English without any formal lessons. 'You will be pleased to issue all Proclamations in English as well as in Italian, and in a few years the latter may be gradually dismissed,' wrote the secretary of state as though the Maltese would become fluent from reading proclamations. Plans were made to teach English in schools, but these fell through when insufficient English teachers were forthcoming.

In a grand gesture, Maitland ordered that advocates and attorneys could practise only if they spoke English; after his death the ruling had to be dropped because too many were being

Page 53: Valletta today, main street.

Page 54: Valletta today, side street.

deprived of their livelihood. Court proceedings took on an almost farcical note :

> . . . the evidence is given in Maltese; the judge dictates it in narrative form to the registrar in Italian, and it is written down in Italian. Then it is read over to the witness, the judge re-translating it orally. The speeches of counsel for the prosecution and defence are in Italian; the judge sums up in Italian to the jury, whose knowledge of that language is by no means certain, and the prisoner, if convicted, is sentenced in Italian . . .

From 1830 a series of attempts was made to revise the islands' legal code. After a good deal of argument on the language question, a commission of Maltese and British judges managed to prepare a draft based largely on the current Neapolitan code. In response to British protests the Colonial Secretary, Lord Glenelg, with a democratic gesture ordered the draft to be published in Malta and to be subject to public debate, forgetting that most Maltese could not read and that public discussion would be taken by them as a sign of weakness.

When the new code had been accepted in principle, discussion continued on matters of detail. A clause governing punishments for offences against religion, ranked all religions equal; but the Maltese pressed for heavier penalties for crimes against the catholic church, while the British demanded a separate clause for crimes against the protestant church. Then the British objected to the catholic church being promoted to *dominante* (principal), only to find that the archbishop did not care for the alternative *chiesa del Paese* (church of the country). And so on. It was 1854 before agreement was reached, the negotiations having taken twenty-four years.

CONSTITUTIONAL MANOEUVRES

Meanwhile, the constitution also was going slowly through a process of change and challenge. An active noble, Camillo

Sceberras, and a busy clerk, George Mitrovich, formed a committee to demand representative institutions. They started with a plea for a freely elected assembly of thirty members but this was rejected, being far more liberal than anything yet granted to a British colony. 'Surely', said the permanent under-secretary of state for the colonies, 'the people of Malta have no wish to meddle with the affairs of Government, or if any do, they are not of the most respectable class.' The best the British could offer was a re-vamped advisory council with seven members, three of whom were to be Maltese—the archbishop, a representative of the landed proprietors, and a representative of the merchants. The archbishop was then banned by Rome from joining because the new oath of office included a clause promising never to 'disturb or weaken the Protestant Religion . . . of the United Kingdom.'

This feeble essay in democracy did not fool anyone, so Sceberras and Mitrovich tried again. In 1836 they resurrected the old case for a *consiglio popolare*, presenting a petition which quite justly pointed out that not only were the islanders banned from an effective say in government, but the lack of a free press and municipal institutions virtually prevented all expressions of opinion.

In reponse to these pressures, another commission was formed, whose British members included John Austin and George Lewis. In his briefing Glenelg said : 'The Comissioner will not fail to bear in mind that there is no part of the Dominions abroad in which the King is more entitled to require of His Servants an habitual discretion of conduct, sobriety of demeanour and mutual forbearance . . .' Lewis, a sympathetic observer aged thirty, wrote copious letters to his father, some of which were later published.

> In many respects the people here, I am sorry to say, remind me of the Irish. They have in common mistrust and mendaciousness among the upper classes, and superstition and prolificness among the lower . . . Starving nobles with fine sounding titles and a couple of hundred pounds a year marry at twenty and beget twelve or

fourteen children. You may judge, with an upper class multiplying in this manner, of the intense hatred with which they regard the English, who fill all the well-paid offices; and of the eagerness with which they look forward to the time when the places will be given to Maltese. The people have contracted such a habit of dependence on the Government that their only notion of improvement in their condition seems to be the multiplication of moderately paid offices to be given to Maltese. The Government, instead of attempting to give the people feelings of self-reliance, have intentionally kept them in a state of pupilage, have discouraged all movement, have stifled all inquiry, have perpetuated ignorance, and have even discountenanced trade as being troublesome.

A CAPRICIOUS ECONOMY

There was certainly much distress in Malta at the time. In quarantine for fourteen years after the 1813 plague, during which period trade was lost to other Mediterranean ports, the Greek War of Independence in 1821 had further upset commerce. Farmers, their rents fixed during the boom years, had found it difficult to compete with lower prices in the cotton and grain markets. Three thousand ships had entered Valletta in 1812; fewer than 1,000 had called in 1826. Agricultural wages had fallen from 1s 6d a day during the boom to about $6\frac{1}{2}$d a day; many workers had been reduced to sleeping out of doors and to living on prickly pears, thistles and clover. There were no unemployment figures but, in 1824, 4,000 men had applied for charitable relief.

Austin and Lewis favoured a consultative council with a property-owning and education franchise, a free press, the extended use of Italian in education, the abolition of sinecures and the appointment of qualified Maltese to higher offices. The colonial secretary, however, had less liberal views.

Austin's wife, an attractive, perceptive woman, made a lasting contribution to the islanders' welfare. 'The moral and intellectual destitution of the people is dreadful,' she wrote.

No schools in the Casals [villages]; no tolerable education for the middling classes; a university whose first professor receives £25 a year and to which no attention is paid by the government; no press, no place for discussion, no intercourse with the English of an amicable and instructive kind. What wonder if they are ignorant and childish? The only thing I *cannot* understand is how life is sustained under such circumstances.

Thanks to her zeal and enthusiasm, by the time she left, ten village schools had started or were about to start.

Maltese hopes had been raised when the commission was appointed; when little practical change resulted, there was naturally a feeling of bitterness. Some small reforms were made. Spending on education went up from £1,725 to £4,000 a year. Public work spending was doubled. The Maltese were given press freedom, subject to strict laws of libel. But little was done to improve the Maltese economy or to provide outlets for Maltese talents and ambitions. The situation was not helped by another cycle of disasters. In 1837 there was a cholera outbreak, and from 1840 to 1841 the islands suffered a severe drought. The wretched condition of agriculture at last persuaded the government to make a belated reform; land rents were lowered by one quarter.

ALOOF AND UNLOVED

Outside influences were not wholly conducive to Anglo-Maltese harmony. In 1839, Dowager Queen Adelaide visited the island for her health and began a vogue for Malta as a health and holiday resort. English visitors increased, among them ardent protestants bent on showing the Maltese the error of their popish ways. Queen Adelaide gave £10,000 for the building of a protestant church, a plan which caused fierce opposition on the islands. Meanwhile, as Italy erupted on its way to unification, refugees fled in large numbers to Malta. They were mainly liberal republicans who encouraged pro-Italian factions to militate against the British on the grounds that the Maltese, being ethnically Italian, ought to be allowed to adopt Italian as their natural language.

Britons based on the islands, and their friends, failed to win love or respect from the Maltese. Aloof, often in overpaid sinecure jobs, they tended to treat Malta trivially, as a cheap way of living the good life. '. . . the Maltese are mostly amphibious, and the lower orders pass half their time in the water,' wrote the Marchioness of Westminster with haughty condescension. 'Sailors love the place,' said another visitor. 'Balls are gay, dinner parties are numerous, horses are fleet, wine is cheap, grog is plentiful, fruit is abundant.'

The British and Maltese would not mix, even at higher levels of society. Lord Hastings, the governor after Maitland,

> . . . endeavoured to promote union by having all parties frequently and unformally at the palace, thus raising the natives in their own estimation; but since his lordship's death, separation again widened. Our customs, diametrically opposed, offer, it must be confessed, a bar to sociality. We dine at six; they dine at two. We associate through the instrumentality of cookery and wine; they are satisfied with simple converzazioni.

Lewis saw it this way.

> Their manners and deportment are, almost without exception, unobjectionable, and very superior to those of some of the vulgar English wives of naval men and Government officers, who find themselves in an unwonted position of power and importance, and therefore think it incumbent on them to trample on the Maltese with all the weight of their vulgarity. If an Englishman is to preserve any vestige of sympathetic feelings towards his own countrymen as such, he should certainly never see them out of England.

The governor's job was never easy and Whitehall sometimes made an unhappy match of the man to the islands. Sir Patrick Stuart, governor through the turblent 1840s, was a strict sabbatarian and a man of rigid outlook. It had for some time been the custom in Malta to hold a carnival on the Sunday before Ash

Wednesday; this, Stuart forbade. An angry crowd gathered, became embroiled with a British regiment and was cleared eventually by the police.

BETTER DAYS

In compensation, the British chose as their next governor a catholic, Sir Richard More O'Ferrall; the Maltese welcomed him also as the first civilian to hold the appointment. Their hopes that he would come to grips with their domestic problems were not entirely disappointed. Among his creations was Malta's chamber of commerce, an influential body which to this day has played a constructive part in the islands' affairs.

But even he could not avoid giving offence. Sicily having turned republican, the King of Naples was engaged in a last grim bloodbath in a vain attempt to keep his throne. There was much sympathy in Malta for refugees from the Naples terror but the Church was afraid of anti-catholic propaganda, and Britain feared complications, were Malta to be used as a base for plots against the King of Naples. So a law was made restricting entry to foreigners who could produce a 'guarantee' from a consul or a 'respectable resident'. When a shipload of refugees next arrived, only a few could produce guarantees, the rest being turned back. O'Ferrall was immediately branded as heartless and cruel.

Britain chose this moment to introduce Malta's first partly-elected legislative council. Set up in 1849, the council comprised eight elected and ten nominated members; as half of the nominated members were Maltese, the islanders predominated. Franchise rested on language (competence in English or Italian) and property. Half the available revenue was to stay in the hands of the governor, the rest being spent by the council.

With the onset of the Crimean War, Malta's trade was on the upswing once again. Naval and military expenditure rose from £200,000 in 1852 to £800,000 in 1856; agricultural and unskilled wages went up by about a half. During the war the governor and the military commander clashed on defence matters; the next governor, Sir John Gaspard le Marchant, also quarrelled with the commander. It was obvious that split control was unworkable and, after le Marchant, the governor once again assumed military control.

Le Marchant was strong enough to tackle some of the abuses that were creeping in. Lack of compulsory retirement in the civil service was blocking its departments with elderly men. An underpaid police force was kept going on bribes. The courts of law were dumping grounds for inefficient officials. Apathy prevailed. A British visitor, talking in 1856 to the eminent lawyer, Dr Adrian Dingli, commented : 'The people have the prejudices, the cautions, the want of enterprise, the petty cares and the narrow views of old age.' Dingli replied : 'Many of those qualities, or of those defects, belong to us not as an old country, but as a little one. I believe that the mind shrinks as the sphere of its activity is circumscribed, and that those who live in a narrow society become narrow-minded.'

During the American Civil War, the island's cotton trade benefited from the disruption across the Atlantic, the price in Valletta rising from 30s a quarter in 1861 to 150s in 1862. By 1863 the acreage under cotton had more than doubled. Towards the end of the sixties, however, cholera caused a setback and Italy began to cream off some of Malta's trade. But the opening of the Suez Canal in 1869 brought the island back into prominence. The dockyard was enlarged and in two years the number of ships passing through Malta increased by a thousand.

THE POWER CONFLICT

In the last thirty years of the nineteenth century, Britain's colonies gained gradual increases in responsibility. But in Malta a little was not enough—the gap between British and Maltese points of view was still wide. 'Malta had applied to be annexed through "the love of the Maltese" and believed she was an autonomous state entering as an independent nation,' writes A. V. Laferla in *British Malta*. Wellington had put the British military viewpoint in a House of Lords debate :

> What is Malta? It is a fortress and a seaport . . . it is a great naval and military arsenal for our shipping and forces in the Mediterranean. We hold it by conquest and by treaty after conquest. We hold it as an important post, as a great military and naval arsenal, and as nothing more.

The Maltese had a nobility as old as the British; they had achieved a form of self-government only a couple of hundred years after Britain's *Magna Carta*; they had ancient links with Italy, progenitor of the Roman Empire and the Renaissance. To be given an elective council but no real power of decision, was tantamount to an insult. In 1864 the Secretary of State, Edward Cardwell, had made a ruling that 'no vote of money should be pressed against the elected majority except under very special circumstances. . .' But in 1873 the governor passed monetary and drainage projects against the votes of the elected members, and he overruled them when a rise in salary for the chief secretary was being debated. The Cardwell ruling looked like trickery and the Maltese retaliated by treating the council with scorn; when opposed by the official members, the elected members walked out. Later they used the even more sardonic weapon of electing idiots to the council.

While both sides wrangled over control of the machine, the machinery itself grew rustier with neglect. A new drainage system was urgently needed, but the estimated cost was £70,000 against the islands' total revenue of only £164,000. By tradition, revenue was raised by taxing necessities such as bread, ignoring property and trade; as a result, the lower classes paid at least as much a head as the middle and upper classes. While British spending in defence went up, no rent was paid for military buildings and establishments.

The elected members lost some claim to have the islands' interests at heart when, nervous of raising extra taxes, they opposed the new drainage plan. The British government sent out a commissioner who suggested new taxes on beer, tonnage dues, storage rent for bonded goods, and a reduced tax on wheat. There was immediate uproar, the Maltese being led to 'make a demonstration against the vexatious measures of the Imperial Government.'

Advisers were at a loss to draw a balance between Maltese and British interests. Patrick Keenan, sent out in 1878 to enquire into education, found a sad state of affairs. Teachers were ill-paid and often ill-educated; students at the university were left to run their own courses; each professor worked independently of the others.

POLITICAL PRESSURES

In the 1880s political and language differences hardened. The British rein was loosened a little in 1881 when an executive council 'to advise and assist the Governor' was formed of three official members of the lower council. Some strong personalities emerged in the political arena and formed themselves gradually into opposing sides; the *riformista* party, which was for linguistic reform, giving dominance to English; and the *anti-riformistas*, who supported Italian. The former was led by Dr Savona who pointed out that under France or Russia the islanders would surely have been forced to make a linguistic concession. The latter, led by Dr Mizzi, emphasized Malta's ties with Italy and played on fears of protestantism.

Another man harrying the British at this time, and destined to play an important part in Maltese history, was Count Strickland. With an English father and Maltese mother he later became both a British parliamentarian and a member of the Maltese council. He

63

was to serve the British as governor of the Leeward Islands, then of Western Australia; and the Maltese as prime minister. He sided at first with the Italianate Mizzi, evolving gradually into a pro-British imperialist.

Agitation for a new constitution was renewed, with Mizzi and Strickland pressing hard for reform. The Maltese efforts were at last rewarded when, in 1887, the colonial secretary said the government's objectives were to 'give the representatives of the people of Malta, for the first time, a specific power of deciding questions of finance and other questions of local concern. . .'

Although the new constitution appeared to be a step forward, it offered the illusion rather than the substance of executive responsibility. As the governor retained the power of veto, the council was like a child playing at democracy under the eye of parents ready to stop the game when it became too rough. Moreover, only about ten thousand people were eligible to vote, and it was computed a few years later that fewer than half this number bothered to do so.

In 1889 there was a positive step towards religious understanding when Britain appointed a special envoy to the Pope. As religious differences subsided, language problems worsened. Trouble began when Strickland was made chief secretary in 1889. Having veered away from his pro-Italian views, a 'betrayal' that aroused bitter opposition, he set about re-organising the schools on the basis that parents could choose between English or Italian instruction for their children. Although a census ten years later was to show 95.4 per cent opting for English and only 4.6 per cent for Italian, the pro-Italian group was loth to give up.

THE WAR OF WORDS

Matters were brought to a head by the affair of Colonel Hewson. An English army officer, he was a witness in an embezzlement case. As was customary in the courts, his evidence was transcribed in Italian. When this was passed to him for approval he refused to sign, on the ground that he could not corroborate something he did not understand. The court imprisoned the colonel for contempt but the governor immediately gave him a free pardon. Simmering hostility erupted into open war, the Maltese resenting direct interference with one of their major institutions. But the British had the whip hand. Joseph Chamberlain, the Colonial Secretary, ordered that English become an optional choice in the courts. When the council retaliated by postponing the education estimates, the British promptly made an order in council that forced the estimates through—and then, rubbing salt in the wound, issued the decree that, in fifteen years. English would be substituted for Italian in *all* court proceedings. The 1887 constitution was now virtually in shreds.

These moves brought Strickland into violent opposition to his former ally, Mizzi, whom he accused of turning Malta into a 'tower of Babel'. Strickland declared that 'the language of this country is Maltese, and the language of the Empire is English.' Mizzi fought back, using his Italian-language newspaper as a weapon of war; he also went to London to petition the colonial secretary for a fully-elected legislative council, an executive council answerable to the legislative council, and a return to Italian in the law courts. Chamberlain retorted that the Italian faction represented only a small part of the population, and that the Maltese generally had failed to take enough interest in the democratic institutions already granted. 'Her Majesty's Government', he said, 'cannot consent to extend a Constitution which, in view of the special circumstances of the island, appears to them to be sufficiently liberal.'

Malta's special situation, as a strategic fortress, was once again becoming important. As the European nations grouped and regrouped into opposing sides, Britain was concerned about its power in the Mediterranean. In particular, it was highly desirable to keep the friendship of Italy, at that time a member of the triple alliance with Germany and Austria. But Italy, interpreting the assault against the Italian language in Malta as a blow to national pride, was ill-disposed towards the British government. Chamberlain made two peace-seeking trips to the Mediterranean. Meanwhile, the elected members of the Maltese council sat on their hands, refusing to pass measures until recognition was given to Mizzi's education ordinance, by which Italian would be the 'medium of instruction and language of communication in every public educational institution.'

On the substitution of English for Italian in the courts, Chamberlain gave in. He hoped, with this concession, that the Maltese council would be quiescent, but while the free-language choice still prevailed in the schools, the Maltese members remained hostile. In 1903, patience on both sides being exhausted, the British brought their ultimate weapon to bear—suspension of the constitution.

PARTY POLITICS...

In the previous year, defence spending in the Maltese Islands had been reduced by £400,000, but construction of a large breakwater at the entrance to Grand Harbour kept employment at a high level until 1906. Then a serious financial crisis hit the island, causing mass unemployment, falling wages and a rising government deficit. The economic situation became so bad that, in 1911, another commission was appointed. The commissioners reached the usual conclusion; that Malta's economy was falsely based. 'A sudden withdrawal of the British fleet and garrison', they said, 'would reduce a large section of the population to idleness and starvation.' But they pointed out also that, with £640,000 in the savings bank, the Maltese generally could hardly be called impoverished. As practical measures they recommended lowering the bread tax, raising the tobacco and liquor tax, investigating government spending and letting Malta off its annual military payment of £5,000.

Under a patched-up constitution, in the years leading up to the

First World War, the elected council members continued their old strategy of abstention and anti-government tirades in the press. In 1915 they acquired a new leader, Enrico Mizzi, son of the former leader of the pro-Italian faction, and no less fiery than his father. International peace at the end of the war did not bring peace to the Maltese political scene; the economy slumped once again and the islands suffered their worst disturbance ever. In 1919, to mark the despatch to London of a new petition for a change of constitution, rioting and looting broke out among the unemployed in Valletta. When the police lost control, troops were called in and three Maltese were killed in the mêlée.

The shock calmed the extremist politicians and jolted the British into mooting a greater degree of independence for the islands. The Maltese, having set up their own unofficial 'national assembly' with representatives from all sections of the community, the British secretary of state agreed in 1921 on a constitution giving them a real measure of control over local affairs. In the following years two main parties emerged : the nationalist party, pro-Italian, basically conservative, supported by the educated classes and led by Mizzi; and the constitutional party, led by Count Strickland, pro-British and influenced towards socialism by its alliance with the labour party.

The nationalists won the first two elections, with the constitutionalists winning the third in 1927, upon which a new battle developed, this time between Strickland and the Church. Ultra-conservative, and linked strongly to Italy, the Church leant naturally towards the nationalists, leading Strickland to assume that the islands' most powerful influence was against him.

Two events brought this unspoken emnity into the open. The government comprised two houses, the legislative and the senate, and bills had to pass through both before they became law. Strickland had drafted a Financial Appropriations Bill, drawing upon money the nationalists had carefully put aside in an emergency fund; the two clerical representatives in the senate sided with the opposition and voted the Bill down. When Strickland protested to the archbishop, the clergy agreed to abstain from voting altogether until peace was restored. Strickland was then reported to have said, 'Certain priests . . . are going to be politically hostile to my Party at the next election and I take this threat as a declaration of war.' Feelings were now so touchy that when a friar was ordered by the Church to leave Malta 'as a matter of discipline', Strickland declared that the friar was being penalised for his support of the constitutional party.

...PETTY POLITICS

Acrimony flared on both sides. A Church investigator reported to the Holy See that 'reliable witnesses do not hesitate to say that at the present moment Malta is being subjected to a reign of terror and despotism.' An apostolic delegate went further, saying that Strickland 'wishes to make the Church subservient to the State.' The British government, having stayed on the touchline, objected strongly that the Holy See 'had declared to be *persona non grata* the head of a responsible Government in a British Colony.' The Vatican, its eye on the 1930 election, declared that the Pope would do all he could 'to put an end to a line of action harmful to Religion.' There was another protest from Britain at this 'outside interference', to which the Maltese archbishop reacted by telling parish priests to steer support away from Strickland. When reports were heard of priests refusing absolution to parishioners favouring the constitutional party, and two Maltese ministers tried to investigate the rumours, it was the Church's turn to object to unwarranted interference. The bishop now gave a clear order to catholics not to vote for Strickland—upon which the islands' privy council pronounced that the whole election be suspended.

As a further blow, doubts were being cast on the legality of the existing Strickland administration. The accusers' case rested on a provision in the constitution for two senate members to be nominated by a 'Trades Union Council'; as such a body did not exist, the governor had given the palm to certain unions considered capable of electing the two members. When it was discovered that some of these unions were bogus, there was a long lawsuit the outcome of which was a ruling that the two senators were illegal. It followed that Bills voted for or against by two illegal senators were themselves illegal, and to prevent nearly three years' legislation being nullified, a letters patent was hastily added to the constitution giving Britain power to make laws touching the general interests of Maltese residents in times of emergency; in effect this meant that the governor's signature made the laws legal. But these reserve powers cancelled out the whole point of the constitution which was intended to give the Maltese control over their own affairs. Thus, suspension of the constitution became inevitable, and in 1931 yet another commission travelled from Britain to Malta.

A year and a half later, passions having cooled, the constitutional party was claiming that the use of Italian was the cause of all the troubles, while the nationalist party was simply insisting that a constitution granted to a catholic country 'could only function in the conditions which, however unintelligible to British opinion, prevail in such countries.' The commission now quietly recommended that the constitution be restored and the election campaign continued where it had been left off.

Strickland apologised for his earlier attack on the Church but the Maltese could not forgive him and the nationalists won the election. With Mizzi as minister of education, Italian influence gradually spread; fascist ideas, then taking hold in Italy, soon followed. The nationalists overstepped the mark by allowing £5,000 in the accounts for teaching Italian; no doubt glad of an excuse to check the spread of Mussolini's propaganda, the British declared a state of emergency and the constitution was suspended once more.

In 1936 the Maltese were given another constitution and this time Italian was officially banished, English being the language for administration, and Maltese in the courts. In 1939 a more liberal constitution was planned as a step towards self-government. But war intervened and the islands' turbulent politics were set aside as a more violent conflict took the stage.

Page 71 : (*left*) Mdina Cathedral, exterior; (*right*) Mdina Cathedral, interior.

Page 72: (above) Village Church at Nadur, Gozo; (below) country house: Gomerino, near Rabat.

4   THE GREATER SIEGE

*To honour her brave people, I award the George Cross to the
Island Fortress of Malta to bear witness to a heroism and devotion
that will long be famous in history.*
15 April 1942   GEORGE RI

THE siege of the Maltese Islands during the Second World
War, in its grimmest phase at the time of this award, is
well known as a sustained defensive battle against cruel
odds. But it was more than this. When Maltese fortunes were at
their lowest ebb and surrender as the alternative to starvation was
only weeks away, the offensive of forces based on these harassed
islands was taking a critical toll of seaborne supplies to Rommel's
forces in North Africa. El Alamein, in the autumn of 1942, was a
great victory not only for the army under Montgomery's brilliant
command; it was Malta's victory too.

An official account of the RAF's work in wartime Malta, published in 1944, said: 'The island was not a single weapon wielded
as an isolated arm: it had an integral part to play in Mediterranean strategy as a whole.' In Churchill's words: 'The heroic
defence of Malta in 1942 formed the keystone of the prolonged
struggle for the maintenance of our position in Egypt and the
Middle East.' Rommel was more specific: 'Malta has the lives of
many thousands of German and Italian soldiers on its conscience.'
More recent evidence comes from Dr Hans-Adolf Jacobsen, the
German historian. In 1967, in a recorded interview, he criticised
Rommel for his decision in the summer of 1942 when, having
reached the El Alamein line, he chose to support Hitler's 'hair-
brained scheme for an immediate breakthrough to Alexandria.'
This plan was the outcome of a controversy which for some
months had divided the German and Italian generals, the main

question having been whether the breakthrough plan should be adopted or whether the Afrika Korps should hold its position on the Egyptian border until seaborne supplies had been secured by the capture of Malta. Rommel's calculation that Malta could wait, proved fatal. Jacobsen said, 'Failure to capture Malta was decisive and led eventually to Rommel's defeat since half of his supplies were destroyed *en route.*'

ASSETS AND LIABILITIES

Little of this could have been known to the bomb-drenched people of Malta during the dark days of 1942. Fortunately they had other consolations. They believed their cause to be just. They had their deeply-ingrained religious faith. They had the steadying leadership of a devout governor, Sir William Dobbie and, from June 1942, of his energetic successor, Viscount Gort. They had their inherent fortitude, the gift of a long history of struggle and privation. Their ordeal was being shared by the sturdy British fighting men in their midst. And their islands had one invaluable natural asset—limestone rock.

Malta's close-packed cities, being built largely of this strong and versatile material, there was little in the structures to catch fire. The material damage inflicted by the air raids was bad enough; it would have been much worse if the ensuing fires had been able to take hold or if the buildings had been of flimsier construction. More important, limestone *in situ* provided the ideal venue for air raid shelters. This rock, easily worked, hardens quickly on exposure to the air. When war came to them, the Maltese lost no time in burrowing into the limestone, creating galleries and networks of caves to supplement the shelter already available to them in old disused ramparts, moats and fortifications. As the first bombs were falling, volunteers went quickly to work with pick-axes improvised in great numbers by the naval dockyard; by the end of the war the number of safe and convenient refuges in the islands exceeded the total population. Thousands of people in Malta today owe their survival to limestone rock.

The first bombs fell on the islands on 11 June 1940, the day after Italy entered the war. Malta was ill-prepared. No fighter protection was available. Only forty anti-aircraft guns could be brought into action. The fleet, which in the safer days of peace had crowded the Maltese harbours, was out of the way in Alexandria. This densely-populated area, barely sixty miles from Sicily, was exposed, virtually naked, to the enemy.

In the pre-war years there had been disagreement among British politicians and the heads of the three fighting services about the value of Malta in war. The Royal Navy, conscious that it had in Malta large-scale dockyard facilities and a base which, besides being vital to the Maltese economy, was a prime asset in the navy's worldwide armoury, considered the Maltese Islands to be vital to Middle East strategy, but needed the help of the army and the RAF to ensure their defence. The army and the RAF considered Malta to be untenable under heavy air attack, and of limited value so long as French territories in North Africa could be used as air staging-points to the east.

Defence policy, as finally adopted, relied absolutely on effective alliance with France. Retaliatory air strikes from France and from the French territories in North Africa would counter air raids on Malta from Italian airfields. It was never envisaged that France would be forced out of the war and that its airfields in Algeria and Tunisia, far from protecting Malta, would fall into enemy hands and become an additional threat to the Maltese Islands.

THE REALITY OF WAR

The fall of France in 1940, followed later by enemy occupation of the greater part of the North African coastline and of Greece,

75

left Malta practically isolated. It needed only the defeat of Malta to give the Axis powers control of all but the eastern and western extremities of the Mediterranean, and the chance to effect a rapid build-up of their armies in North Africa into a force whose advance towards the Suez Canal and the Middle Eastern oil fields would have proved irresistible.

When war came to Malta, Britain, now fighting the Axis powers almost single-handed, its own situation desperate, lost no time in sending supplies and reinforcements. The monitor *Terror*, with her heavy armament, was anchored off Valletta to give anti-aircraft support to the batteries ashore, and towards the end of June the first trickle of Hurricane fighters reached the islands. Supply ships continued to unload their cargoes; in September a large convoy, the first of several, arrived safely with major reinforcements.

Meanwhile, the British forces stationed on the islands, the civil authorities and the Maltese themselves had not been inactive. As the first bombs were bursting around Valletta, an urgent signal was on its way to Alexandria seeking approval to retain for Malta's defence the contents of some crates lying in a Maltese warehouse in transit to the Middle East. The crates contained the parts of four Gladiator aircraft. These bi-planes were quickly assembled, flying-boat pilots offered their services, and Malta's fighter defence was in business. For nearly three weeks the Gladiators fought an incessant battle in the skies against the waves of Italian bombers. One of the four was soon destroyed but the surviving three, christened affectionately *Faith*, *Hope* and *Charity* by the admiring people of Malta, fought on until the more modern and effective Hurricanes reached the islands to take over their role.

The early air attacks took the form of high-level precision bombing by Italian planes flying in formation, with the naval dockyard and the airfields as their main targets. Despite the acute shortage of equipment and supplies to ensure its own defence, Malta without hesitation assumed an offensive role. Bombs from Malta-based aircraft were soon causing damage and dislocation to enemy airfields and shipping, while reconnaissance flights from Maltese airfields began to yield a regular flow of information about enemy movements on land and sea. In the autumn of 1940, on the strength of accurate reports by RAF reconnaissance aircraft, torpedo bombers of the Royal Navy struck a crippling blow at the Italian fleet lying in Taranto. This major victory, and the existence at that time of Allied air bases in Libya, made it possible for east-to-west convoys to play their part in the relief of Malta, a supply route that was to become untenable later on. The air reconnaissance effort was maintained right through the war, playing a crucial part in Allied plans and actions. Malta's invaluable role as a refuelling halt for aircraft bound to and from Britain and the Middle East was also maintained throughout the war years.

In the late summer of 1940, the Italians turned from high-level to dive bombing attacks but by November, when further war supplies in large quantities reached Valletta by convoy, Italian air attacks began to fall off in the face of tougher and more penal resistance by Maltese defences. Aircraft based on the islands were now markedly stepping up their offensive and Axis convoys from Europe to North Africa were beginning to suffer losses.

THE BLITZ DEVELOPS

In the enemy's view this was not good enough and at the turn of the year the Luftwaffe was sent south to stiffen the waning Italian air assault. In January 1941 German bombers, pressing home their attacks with vigour and determination, began to make a serious mark on Malta and its defences. The arrival in Valletta of the aircraft-carrier *Illustrious*, damaged by enemy air attacks while escorting a convoy from Alexandria, was the signal for seven days of sustained onslaught by dive bombers. The attacks concentrated on the wounded carrier at her repair berth and caused severe damage to the dockyard and to the crowded cities in its vicinity. *Illustrious*, whose destruction was the prime object of the assault, survived and was able to make her way back to Alexandria. This savage blitz marked the start of the real siege of the Maltese Islands; it was to last until November 1942, a period of nearly two years.

During the first five months of 1941, the Luftwaffe went all out to render Malta untenable. Supplies continued to arrive by sea at the cost of heavy losses to the convoys bringing them. Malta's defence by fighters and anti-aircraft batteries was maintained despite the interruptions caused by bomb damage to airfields and communications. Maltese soldiers manned the guns side by side with their British comrades. Air strikes and reconnaissance flights from Malta were kept up. Light naval forces, which had been built up slowly during the previous months, operated regularly from Maltese harbours against enemy shipping. In April 1941, four British destroyers from Malta attacked and sank an entire Axis convoy comprising five supply ships and their four supporting warships. British submarines, which lay submerged in the deep water of Maltese harbours during the heavier air attacks, played an active part in distant waters, while minesweepers worked to keep the harbour approaches clear for shipping.

But as spring approached, the incessant enemy air attacks, taking their toll, gradually began to gain the upper hand. Then in May 1941 came temporary relief; the Luftwaffe was withdrawn from this theatre of war to Hitler's new Russian front. The Italian air force, however, continued its air attacks on Malta throughout the summer and autumn of that year and, in July, the Italian navy made a gallant but fruitless assault on the fortress with E-boats, all of which were sunk or driven off by the islands' coastal batteries.

At the end of the year the Germans returned to the attack with a vengeance. Kesselring, having been appointed in command of the Axis area in southern Europe, with his headquarters in Sicily was able to augment his existing forces, part German and part

Italian, with a Luftwaffe air group transferred from the Russian front. This move gave him 2,000 first-line planes. His prime object was to gain control of the air and of the sea between southern Italy and North Africa, thereby ensuring safety of communications through Libya and Cyrenaica to the Afrika Korps. Neutralisation of the Maltese bastion was a key factor of this strategy.

A LULL BEFORE THE STORM

Fortunately for Malta, exceptionally bad weather during the early months of 1942 hindered the enemy air assault. At the same time it caused a dramatic relief of Malta-based attacks on enemy supply ships. Whereas less than one-third of Axis shipping from Italy had been getting through to North Africa towards the end of 1941, by February 1942 more than two-thirds were succeeding. Furthermore, with the capture of Benghazi by Axis forces in January 1942, Allied fighter bases in that area, which had helped to protect Malta-bound convoys, now became enemy bomber bases. The fall of Crete completed the encirclement of Malta, and the concentration of enemy forces around the central Mediterranean basin made an immediate and almost lethal impact on the Maltese supply position.

It became particularly expensive in men and ships to sail the east-to-west convoys from Alexandria. In January 1942 three out of four convoyed supply ships reached Malta from Egypt, but in February a similar convoy failed entirely to get through. Three supply ships, escorted by a cruiser and eight destroyers and with a supporting force of two cruisers and eight destroyers, were heavily attacked from the air, and none of the three ships reached Malta.

In the following months four supply ships, including a naval tanker, left Alexandria for Malta. Their escort was stepped up to four cruisers and sixteen destroyers, to be augmented at the approaches to Malta by another cruiser based temporarily at Valletta. This force, besides continuous air assault, was attacked by an Italian squadron comprising a battleship, three cruisers and ten destroyers. The Italians were driven off at the cost of damage to some of the British destroyers, and one of the supply ships was sunk. The three survivors reached Malta only to be sunk by bombers while unloading their urgent cargoes. Less than one-quarter of their much needed supplies were salved. The cruiser *Penelope*, which had gone out from Malta to support this convoy, was damaged by air attack and, while under repair in the naval dockyard, became the target for a prolonged series of dive bombing strikes. Riddled with holes, she was christened 'Pepperpot' by the Maltese, whose sense of humour remained intact. But the valiant efforts by naval and civilian repair staffs, working under highly dangerous and almost intolerable conditions, saved the day and, like the *Illustrious* before her, *Penelope* slipped out of the harbour one dark night and made her escape.

This event, and clearer weather over Malta, marked the opening of the most critical phase of the battle for the islands. In March and April the air onslaught on Malta reached a new peak of intensity. During these two months the islands suffered more than twice the weight of bombs which fell in London during the whole of its worst year. In the six months to the end of June 1942, with the exception of one 24-hour period, air raids on Malta were a daily occurrence. On average, three heavy raids took place every day, the most severe of them involving several hundred bombers and escorting fighters. Maltese defences took a heavy toll of the raiders, nearly 200 enemy planes being shot down during April. But the price was high. More fighters were being destroyed on the ground than could be replaced. East-to-west convoys from Alexandria could no longer get through. Apart from a few minesweepers, the naval forces, including the submarine flotilla, were obliged to quit the islands.

The award of the George Cross lifted the spirits of the

beleaguered garrison and of the stoic Maltese people, reminding them that they were not forgotten, that their battle was one with Britain's. But it was difficult not to feel alone. There was no clear road to victory. While Spitfire reinforcements in May led to a temporary easing of the air raids, a new sense of dread was imparted by reconnaissance reports that on Sicilian airfields preparations were being made to invade Malta.

BACKS TO THE WALL

The continued harassment of seaborne supplies to North Africa by Malta-based forces, and the bombers' failure to bring the Maltese people to heel, led the enemy to consider other means of eliminating the islands. The Axis high command worked out a plan for the capture of Malta, using German paratroopers, Italian commandos and barge-borne assault troops. The invasion was scheduled for June 1942. At the eleventh hour, two factors led to cancellation of the plan. Rommel insisted that diversion of these forces to his own command in North Africa would be the quickest and surest way to Suez; and the Italians, nervous of failure, asserted that the available forces were insufficient for the task. It was decided instead to intensify even further the air attacks on Malta, and if these failed totally to subjugate the islands, they should at least nullify Malta-based offensives against Axis supplies to North Africa during the most critical phases of Rommel's advance.

Malta's position in the summer of 1942 was, in a sense, a microcosm of the desperate global situation facing the Allies at that time. While Malta was fighting for its life under vicious and sustained air attack, was facing the possibility of invasion, and was suffering acute shortages of food and weapons, Britain was reeling under a succession of staggering blows in almost every theatre of war. In just over six months, three million tons of Allied shipping had been sunk in the Atlantic by U-boats. Under British noses, the *Scharnhorst, Gneisenau* and *Prinz Eugen* sailed boldly up the English Channel from Brest to the relative security of bases in their homeland. Defeats in Malaya, Burma and the East Indies had brought the Japanese to the frontiers of India. The Indian Ocean was virtually under the control of the Japanese navy. In Russia, the Germans were preparing their decisive attacks on Moscow and Stalingrad. Severe losses were being suffered by the Allied convoys to Russia. In the Aegean, Crete had fallen. In North Africa, Tobruk had been taken and Rommel's armies were only thirty-five miles from Alexandria.

But Churchill's determination to succour Malta never wavered. In June, a major two-pronged effort was mounted to relieve the islands. Each prong consisted of a substantial and heavily-escorted convoy, one approaching from Gibraltar and the other, despite all the dangers, from Alexandria. Seventeen supply ships were assembled for this operation. The combined convoy escorts amounted to eight cruisers and thirty-seven destroyers supported by a battleship, two aircraft carriers, two cruisers and eight destroyers.

Both convoys were vigorously attacked on their respective passages towards Malta. The eastbound convoy from Gibraltar took the brunt of assaults by Italian warships, waves of bombers and a newly-laid minefield off Malta. Two supply ships got through. The westbound convoy from Alexandria, having suffered attacks by U-boats, E-boats and bombers, heavily mauled and its ammunition almost expended, was obliged to retire in the face of almost certain annihilation by an Italian squadron. No supply ships from this convoy reached Malta. The cost of this operation, which brought a mere 15,000 tons of supplies to Valletta, was one cruiser, five destroyers and six supply ships sunk, and several warships and supply ships damaged. Against this, however, could be set the destruction by Malta-based submarines and aircraft of one Italian cruiser and damage to one battleship and a destroyer.

STARVATION — OR SURRENDER?

The almost total failure of these convoys struck a savage blow at Malta's chances of survival. Belts which already pinched, had to be tightened further. That summer, Maltese civilians in their shattered towns and villages carried on at near-starvation levels of rationing. Flour, rice, olive oil, milk, sugar, jam and beer were practically unobtainable. The shops were bare of crockery, cosmetics, and other everyday commodities. Few potatoes or vegetables could be bought. Meat and fish could be obtained only on the black market. The ration of fats and cheese was about one-third that of the equivalent rations allowed in Britain. The coffee ration in Malta was smaller than the British tea ration. Each Maltese had to manage with a quarter of a pound of soap weekly, and barely enough water for basic washing and drinking. Smokers had to make do with two packets of cigarettes a week, leather footwear was almost unobtainable and a reel of cotton, to repair tattered clothing, cost ten shillings.

Even worse, kerosene, the customary domestic fuel in the islands, was in acutely short supply; there was enough for cooking or for light and heat, but not for both. Simple family meals were being cooked on camp fires in the rubble-strewn streets. Victory kitchens struggled to supply each civilian with at least one hot meal a day, but meat, when available, was often goat. Malta depended for existence on the balanced cargoes of three large ships each month, but less than half of this essential flow was being maintained.

At this time, after the failure of the June convoys, the responsible officials in Valletta were, for the first time, obliged secretly to draw up tentative plans for capitulation. At their monthly meetings the governor, the deputy governor and the heads of the fighting services, having assessed the stocks and the prospects of further supplies of essential food, fuel, ammunition and weapons, would calculate the crisis date. If it came to the worst, it had to be surrender or slow death by starvation. At the end of June the authorities concluded that the Maltese Islands would have to be surrendered at the beginning of September unless one important convoy, scheduled provisionally for August, could get through to Valletta.

While the supply ships forming this convoy were assembling at Greenock, and part of the naval escort was gathering at Scapa Flow, a welcome shaft of light relieved the darkness of Malta's plight. During July, the fighter strength based on the islands increased enough to make a serious dent in the Luftwaffe's offensive, now at its peak. As the fighters achieved daytime mastery of the sky over Malta, the enemy onslaught wavered. But the shortage of essential supplies, including aviation spirit, was becoming acute, and in a matter of weeks the best efforts of the defending forces must surely fail.

OPERATION 'PEDESTAL'

The August convoy was planned as a major battle. Under the code name 'Pedestal', fourteen supply ships with 85,000 tons of cargo, enough to keep the islanders going for nearly four months, were to have naval and air protection of unprecedented strength. There was to be a covering force consisting of two battleships, three cruisers and fourteen destroyers; an aircraft carrier support force of three carriers deploying seventy fighter aircraft, with an escort of five destroyers; and a convoy close escort comprising four cruisers and eleven destroyers. Each of these forces was to be commanded by a flag-officer. Another aircraft carrier was to accompany the convoy part of the way and return home after flying off thirty-eight Spitfires to reinforce the Malta-based squadrons—and to provide extra cover for the convoy during its approaches to Valletta.

The supporting forces allocated specially by the Malta high command to cover 'Pedestal' included 136 fighters, thirty-eight bombers, sixteen reconnaissance aircraft and a flotilla of submarines on a patrol line to the east of Malta. From Middle East bases, long-range bombers were to harry enemy airfields threatening the convoy. In addition, the enemy's attention was to be diverted by a feint operation in the form of a mock convoy sailing from Alexandria in the direction of Malta. This convoy was to consist of four supply ships, escorted by five cruisers and fifteen destroyers; it was to turn round and go back to Egypt after having made its point.

The 'Pedestal' supply ships were to be loaded with diesel fuel, kerosene, petrol, ammunition and flour. The most vital part of the cargo was to be carried in the American-built tanker *Ohio*, manned by a British crew. Of the other thirteen supply ships, two were to be American-manned and the rest British. All the escorting and support forces were to be British.

Although every effort was made to maintain secrecy, it was inevitable that enemy agents would become aware of such large-scale preparations, and information leaked to Axis sources soon enough for the Germans and Italians to deploy strong forces in 'Pedestal's' path. The enemy opposition comprised 280 German and Italian bombers, including ninety torpedo bombers, and 200 fighters, operating from Sardinia and Sicily; six Italian cruisers, eleven Italian destroyers and twenty-three Italian and German E-boats to await the convoy off Pantelleria; three German U-boats and eighteen Italian submarines on the convoy's route to the east of Gibraltar; and a specially-laid minefield in the narrow waters off Cape Bon.

'Pedestal' sailed according to plan, bringing its forces of warships up to strength at the western approaches to Gibraltar with units from Freetown and Gibraltar. On the night of 10/11 August 1942, this great armada moved silently, under cover of fog, through the Straits of Gibraltar. By ill luck it was spotted by

Spanish fishing boats, whose radio reports confirmed 'Pedestal's' movements to the enemy; and next morning, when the convoy was sixty miles south of Ibiza, an Italian submarine reported its constitution, course and speed.

ACTION STATIONS

The enemy struck his first blow at 13.00 hours that day when, to the north of Algiers, one of the aircraft carriers was sunk outright by a German U-boat's salvo of torpedoes, and with the carrier went a quarter of the convoy's own air cover. At dusk, enemy aircraft made their first attack with dive bombers and torpedo bombers, but no hits were scored. Next morning, 12 August, a second air attack took place, this time by high level bombers; again there were no hits. Shortly afterwards a U-boat attack was driven off. At noon however, the third air attack succeeded in sinking one supply ship with circling torpedoes, a weapon not previously experienced in the war at sea. In the afternoon, by way of retribution, an Italian submarine was rammed by an escorting destroyer and sunk.

With the approach of darkness, as 'Pedestal' cleared Bizerta and entered the narrows between Cape Bon and Skerki Bank, the enemy onslaught began in earnest. The convoy, hemmed in by shallow waters yet still occupying over thirty square miles of sea, was very vulnerable. In two further air attacks that evening, mainly by dive bombers and torpedo bombers, two supply ships and one destroyer were sunk and one supply ship and an aircraft carrier were damaged. During the same period, a submarine attack on the convoy sank one cruiser and damaged another, and the tanker *Ohio*, on which Malta's life depended, was damaged too.

After nightfall, having fulfilled their appointed tasks, the covering force and the aircraft carrier support force withdrew towards Gibraltar. The convoy, confused and partly scattered after the evening's attacks, and now defended only by its close escort, received word at midnight that the Italian navy would attack them at dawn. But there was to be no rest for the harassed ships and their weary crews. A series of E-boat and submarine attacks in the early hours of 13 August sank one cruiser and four supply ships (including the two Americans) and damaged a cruiser and one supply ship. Shortly before dawn, to the south of Pantelleria, the depleted armada, now reduced to seven supply ships (three of them damaged) and an escort of two cruisers and seven destroyers, steeled itself for the naval attack which, if pressed home, could result only in its complete annihilation.

But the gods were merciful. During the night the Italian cruiser squadron, steaming quietly along the coast of Sicily towards its rendezvous, received orders to return to its base to avoid the threat of severe air attacks from Malta-based aircraft. Air attacks there would surely have been, but the threat was greatly exaggerated by an inspired piece of British bluff, and the Italian warships, far from mauling the approaching convoy, ran into a British submarine patrol and suffered serious damage to two cruisers. At dawn, 'Pedestal' was not only spared its duel with the Italian navy; it was now within range of fighters operating from Maltese airfields and could expect cover to a reasonable extent, first by Beaufighters and later by Spitfires. These tireless fighters, covering the final stage of the convoy's passage, flew over 400 sorties.

THE 'OHIO' SAGA

Even so, 'Pedestal' was not to proceed unscathed. During the morning of 13 August there were three further enemy attacks, in the course of which one supply ship was sunk, another damaged and *Ohio* badly lacerated. At noon, the convoy was less than a hundred miles from Valletta but still had a very long way to go.

By now, only three supply ships, with two cruisers and five destroyers, formed the body of the convoy; five destroyers were on detached duties, escorting stragglers and searching for survivors. There were three stragglers including *Ohio*, all of them damaged; *Ohio*, low in the water, was drifting helplessly, temporarily abandoned.

That afternoon the enemy made repeated efforts to dispose of *Ohio*; although she received further damage from dive bombers, this strongly-built ship stayed afloat. A force of minesweepers from Malta now took over convoy escort duties, and most of the surviving ships of 'Pedestal's' original close escort force retired westward. At 18.30 hours, the three undamaged supply ships entered Valletta harbour, to receive a tumultuous welcome from the Maltese people crowding the ramparts.

But the fight for *Ohio* had yet to be settled. During the evening and throughout the long night, her back breaking and her engines and steering gear out of commission, the tanker resisted repeated efforts by the escorting warships to take her in tow. The exhausted crews were frustrated time and again by *Ohio*'s unwieldly and meandering bulk. Meanwhile, one of the other two stragglers was sunk by dive bombers. But the survivor, creeping quietly through the calm seas under her own fighter escort, was more fortunate; she arrived safely in Valletta during the morning of 14 August.

That same morning soon after dawn, *Ohio*, with her escort of two destroyers, four fleet minesweepers and several coastal craft, and under a constant fighter umbrella, was at last taken in tow. Malta was only fifty miles away but enemy dive bombing attacks continued to inflict damage on the stricken tanker whose decks were now almost awash. At 16.00 hours, Valletta was in sight; then at 19.00 hours, as *Ohio* turned a corner off the Maltese coast to enter the narrow channel between the minefields, her tow parted. Despite the efforts of tugs from Malta, augmenting the efforts of the faithful warships, it seemed only a matter of time

Page 89: Fort
St Angelo.

Page 90: (left) Night before: Manoel Theatre; (right) morning after: Auberge d'Aragon.

before *Ohio* would strike a mine and sink within hailing distance of her destination. As though she had not suffered enough, U-boats and E-boats tried to harry her but the these attacks were driven off for the most part by furious fire from Malta's coastal batteries.

The crippled tanker wallowed helplessly in the calm waters off Malta right through that desperate night, but at dawn on 15 August, towing was successfully resumed and at 08.00 hours *Ohio* entered Grand Harbour to a resounding chorus of cheers from the assembled crowds. Malta was saved.

The tanker's precious cargo was unloaded without delay into two local tankers, under the protection of continuous fighter patrols. Meanwhile, the cargoes of the other surviving supply ships were being rapidly dispersed. It had been an expensive operation. 'Pedestal's' losses were one carrier, two cruisers, one destroyer and nine supply ships sunk; one carrier, two cruisers, four destroyers and two supply ships damaged. The enemy losses comprised about forty aircraft shot down, one submarine sunk, two cruisers damaged, and several E-boats sunk or damaged. But it was 'Pedestal's' victory. The object had been achieved. Five supply ships had got through, including the gallant *Ohio*, and Malta could fight on.

TOWARDS VICTORY

The air attacks from Malta on enemy convoys taking supplies to Rommel's armies now became so effective that these vessels were forced to abandon the direct routes to North Africa and take the long way round down the Greek coast. The islanders were still short of supplies; the worst of their battle was over but it had not yet been finally won. As the date of the El Alamein conflict approached, the Axis air forces once again increased the intensity of their air attacks on Malta in a frantic attempt to relieve the pressure on their vital convoys. This further ordeal was borne by

F

the long-suffering Maltese people in the expectation that relief could not be far away.

In November of that critical year, as Montgomery's victorious army advanced westward, the Allied landings in French North Africa took place. As the pincer movement developed, enemy airfields along the North African coast succumbed so that Allied air power reigned once again over the convoy routes to Malta. That month a large convoy from Alexandria reached Valletta intact and the long, hard-fought siege was broken.

The islanders had paid a high price for their bravery. By the end of 1942, over 3,000 Maltese civilians had been killed or seriously injured; that is, one in ninety of the population. 14,000 tons of bombs, during over 3,000 air raid alerts, had destroyed or severely damaged more than 25,000 buildings, including many of historical or architectural importance. But the enemy, in his attacks on these islands, had lost over 1,000 planes, a quarter of them by anti-aircraft fire—almost one plane for each civilian killed. British aircraft losses amounted to just over 500 aircraft of which nearly half had been destroyed on the ground.

So ended Malta's greater siege and, with it, Axis chances of final victory. The tide was now turning in favour of the Allies. Malta's role as a defence base continued but the agony of the Maltese people was over. During 1943, the islanders were visited by their king and by Churchill, Roosevelt and Eisenhower. In the summer, Valletta became the base and springboard for the Allies' successful invasion of Sicily. In August, when Italy capitulated, the Maltese were not denied their moment of triumph; the act of surrender of the Italian navy was staged for all to see right 'under the guns of Malta'.

In 1944, as the centre of gravity of the war in Europe reached northward, the strategic value of the Maltese Islands declined. By the summer of 1945 when first the Germans, and soon afterwards the Japanese, surrendered to the Allies, Malta was resuming its pre-war role as a training and repair base and garrison for British forces. Amid the healing scars of battle, the Maltese people seemed bent cheerfully along familiar peacetime paths. But under the surface, new needs and old ambitions were stirring, and another chapter in the islanders' long struggle for self-determination was about to be written.

5   TOWARDS INDEPENDENCE

A T the end of the Second World War, despite the heavy price paid in loss of life and damage to property, the Maltese economy looked quite healthy. Capital had accumulated, imports had been low and wages had risen steadily. But the air of prosperity disguised the same deep-rooted lack of stability that had been Malta's downfall time and again in the nineteenth century. In an economy geared mainly to the occupying power's defence needs, another wartime boom was to prove only transitory; once more the authorities and the Maltese people were to be taken by surprise.

During the first years of peace there was enough reconstruction work to fend off unemployment. The flow of money from Britain continued, partly for the repair and support of inflated base facilities, and partly towards the cost of the islands' rehabilitation. But Malta lacked industries to provide new employment and long-term stability. While there was still a role for Malta as a British Mediterranean base, the advent of nuclear warfare and the creation of NATO were bound to diminish it. The Maltese people, no longer the 'coveted islanders' of history, faced a new struggle for economic self-sufficiency.

OPENING GAMBITS

The renewed quest for political independence, which soon absorbed much of the energy of Maltese politicians, tended at first to obscure and deflect the islands' economic priorities. Political independence, an emotional and relatively clear-cut issue, offered a familiar and more convenient stick with which to beat the British.

94

Earlier plans for internal self-government had been shelved during the war and, in 1943, the British had promised to revive them when hostilities ended. The outcome was a Maltese national assembly which, together with a commission sent out from Britain, worked out the form of a new constitution. This came into force in 1947; under it Malta was to have an elected legislative assembly with forty members from among whom the prime minister and the cabinet were to be appointed. But the assembly's powers were not to extend to certain areas of policy which were to remain the governor's prerogative. These reserved matters, which included defence, civil aviation, immigration, currency and nationality, were destined to be the cause of many disputes between the Maltese and British governments.

The first elections under this constitution returned the Malta labour party for the first time. Led by Sir Paul Boffa, it had an overwhelming majority. During the next eight years, however, the story was one of disagreements and political uncertainty. Boffa resigned after two years in office and the labour party split. Boffa then headed a new party, the Malta workers' party, while the original labour party, now led by Dominic Mintoff, remained in power until the elections in 1950. This time the nationalist party won, but only just, and within three months the prime minister died, to be succeeded by Dr George Borg Olivier. In 1951 Borg Olivier strengthened his position by combining with the Malta workers' party. Even so, further elections in 1953 failed to give him a really decisive victory.

In 1953 Malta became HQ of the NATO Mediterranean Command, and in the same year a proposal was put forward by the nationalists that Malta should attain dominion status. The British government refused on the grounds that Malta had not attained enough self-sufficiency. Then, before all-party talks could start in London, the Maltese labour party, under Dom Mintoff, resumed power following the 1955 elections.

Later that year, in London, although there were many points

95

on which the British and Maltese delegations could agree, questions about the ultimate status of the Maltese Islands caused much dispute. Malta's labour party wanted some form of integration, with representatives of the Maltese government sitting at Westminster; the nationalist party sought complete independence for Malta within the Commonwealth. Having agreed that decisions on defence and foreign affairs must remain in the hands of the British parliament, it was decided to seek the views of the Maltese people before making a final decision on integration. A referendum held in 1956 showed that nearly half the population supported the integration proposals. Many nationalists boycotted the referendum but, as a clear majority of the votes cast were in favour, the British government accepted the integration plan. In 1958, however, a British proposal for a five-year trial period without representation was rejected and the talks broke down completely.

THE GOAL IN SIGHT

There were other reasons for the growing tensions in Anglo-Maltese relations. In 1955 it had been agreed by both governments that the Maltese economy needed diversification in order to reduce dependence on service expenditure. In 1957 the British minister of defence stated that the run-down of the British services, which was economically necessary for Britain, would inevitably decrease the numbers of men employed in the docks and other establishments in Malta. The Maltese grew more and more uneasy. Dom Mintoff demanded guarantees concerning the Maltese employment level, threatening to abrogate all agreements with Britain unless they were given.

In April 1958 Mintoff's government resigned after disputes about control of the police force. This was a key issue in the islands since, in the absence of a local government structure, the police carried out important administrative functions in the villages. Borg Olivier refused to form a caretaker government in place of the labour party. Demonstrations took place and public discontent increased. The governor, declaring a state of emergency, took over the administration. In 1960 a commission under Sir Hilary Blood was appointed to make recommendations for a new Maltese constitution. The report proposed complete self-government subject to consultation with Britain on certain questions, with a British right of veto in the event of disagreement. The new constitution was accepted with some misgivings and came into operation in 1962.

The nationalist party won the elections in February of that year and Borg Olivier formed a government. His party gained twenty-five seats in the assembly against the labour party's sixteen. But neither party was happy with the new constitution, and independence once again became a live issue. In August Borg Olivier applied formally for independence and talks were opened the following summer. As the two main Maltese parties now desired independence, the British government accepted this as the wish of the majority. But agreement could not at first be reached on various matters including the question of Commonwealth membership, the status of the Church and whether to become a monarchy or a republic.

In the end, having agreed a draft formula, it was decided to hold another referendum by which the Maltese people would be asked : 'Do you approve the proposed constitution for independence?' Sixty-six thousand were found to be in favour and 55,000 against, while 36,000 abstained or spoiled their ballot papers. After more negotiations in London, there was final agreement on the detailed form of the constitution and on questions of aid and defence. It was resolved that British forces would be able to remain in Malta until 1974 and that, over the same ten-year period, Britain would provide £51 million for development and diversification of the economy. And so, at last, the Maltese Islands became independent on 21 September 1964.

TOWARDS INDEPENDENCE

THE CHURCH IN POLITICS

In the thirties, differences between the Strickland government and the Church had led to the refusal of absolution to anyone supporting the constitutional party, a severe penalty for the conscientious catholic. In 1955 a new struggle came to the fore, this time between the Church and the labour party. The first move occurred when the labour party put forward its plans for integration with Britain. This measure threatened a substantial loss of influence for the Church in the field of education, and the Church authorities saw this loss as the thin end of the wider wedge implied by integration with a protestant power.

The labour party was growing rapidly in strength and popularity. In the urban areas it was supported strongly by skilled and semi-skilled workers while in the villages, although the people were more conservative, the agricultural workers were among the most under-privileged of the islands' inhabitants. The labour party established branches under local committees in all those communities where previously there had been no such political apparatus. The priest was traditionally the community leader and he was supported more or less by the police in the role of local 'authority'; thus discussion tended to be confined to affairs of the village through the medium of various secular and religious clubs, particularly the popular 'band' clubs. A petition could be passed to a central government authority through the village canvasser for the local parliamentary candidate, a procedure often open to bribery and of little use to anyone known to be in opposition to the party holding power at the time. The new labour party committees accepted requests from all-comers and their impartiality inspired confidence. The labour government gained further ground with its measures for improved conditions for the under-privileged, including its extensions of the social services.

Inevitably, the churchmen felt that the labour party was trespassing on their preserves and leading people away from the

98

Church. As the bitterness increased an anti-clerical feeling in the labour party grew more articulate, the Church retaliated with accusations that the party had associations with communism and intended to secularise the islands.

Of the six parties fighting the 1962 elections, the labour party was the only one which omitted to declare its loyalty to the Church. The archbishop placed the labour party executive under the canon penalty of interdiction and banned the reading or distribution of the party's publications. Many labour sympathisers, fearful of committing a mortal sin, found themselves in an intolerable dilemma. Then, a few days before the elections took place, the archbishop, in a pastoral letter, advised the people not to vote for the labour party because its programme was 'manifestly socialist and against the Church,' an action that cost the labour party an untold number of votes. The conflict is not yet over; despite more recent appearances to the contrary, such strongly opposed forces in Maltese politics can hardly co-exist without further confrontations.

ECONOMIC DEVELOPMENT

In economic affairs, 1957 was a turning point. This was the year when the British government made its first crucial declaration about the run-down of the services. There was already considerable anxiety about the employment situation, following the gradual decline of the construction industry. These events brought into focus the islands' dire need to develop new industries and earn more from exports. Good intentions evolved fairly quickly into a programme of action and, in 1959, the first Maltese five-year plan was launched.

The total fund for this plan was £32 million, of which the British government agreed to provide £29 million. The three main aims were to convert the docks to commercial use, to expand and diversify industry with the emphasis on production of goods for

99

export, and to encourage tourism. A scheme was devised to attract new industrial ventures. Under it, the new Aid to Industries Board was to scrutinise applications for aid, and any approved enterprise was to be eligible for one or more of five concessions : an income tax holiday for up to ten years; exemption for a specified period from customs duties on capital equipment and raw materials; capital grants not exceeding one-third of the total amount required by the applicant; financial loans; and ready-built factories or serviced sites leased at a subsidised rent.

During the five years of this plan, seventeen purpose-built factories came into being and a fully-serviced industrial estate was completed at Marsa. But some of the new industries proved to be predominantly employers of female labour and the impact on the male unemployment problem was disappointing. This factor was to be taken more seriously into account during the second five-year plan. Other industries set up under the first plan miscalculated their prospects, one notable example being the Rambler car-assembly plant installed in a large factory in the Marsa area. This business collapsed, jobs were lost, money was wasted and, more important, confidence was undermined.

Before the publication of the second plan, Wolfgang F. Stolper came to Malta at the head of a UN technical assistance team, the resulting report being published in 1962. Emphasising the dangers of conservatism in Maltese economic policy, this report argued that funds from Britain should be used less to preserve the industrial *status quo* and more to stimulate innovation and diversification. It called for transformation of the Maltese economic and industrial structure and, in particular, for greater concentration on the production of goods for export, more attention to management training and a stronger drive to increase labour productivity. These recommendations influenced the form of the second five-year plan.

For this second plan, covering the period 1964-1969, £38 million were set aside. Much of this came out of the £51 million which the British government had promised to make available to the Maltese over the ten years following independence. In this plan, a larger proportion of the available funds was allocated to industrial development, tourism and agriculture, while a lesser proportion was to be spent on the docks. Industries would be favoured which might help to absorb men made redundant by the run-down of the services. There were to be more incentives for investment in local industry, and grants to new enterprises would be replaced to a large extent by interest-free loans. By these means, it was hoped to attract only the more efficient firms while reducing the drain on government resources. A Development Corporation was created to consider how these resources could be used to best advantage, and a Board of Standards was set up to influence the quality of industrial products.

Three years after the start of the second five-year plan, when the British government felt obliged to accelerate its programme for the run-down of the services, a joint mission was formed under Lord Robens. This mission's report, published in 1967, was concerned mainly with questions of employment. In confirming the need to create extra jobs for men, it called for more careful manpower planning and for more extensive training and re-training facilities for workers. The report, noting the rapid growth of the tourism industry, warned that zoning and other controls were necessary to ensure that best use was made of limited land and amenities. The success achieved by this industry was well deserved, but over-hasty expansion in future would be self-defeating.

The nature and intentions of the five-year development plans are important considerations when assessing the progress and prospects of individual industries in the islands. The general aims, based on sound priorities, show promise of fulfilment; these are to ameliorate the unemployment situation, to increase both visible and invisible exports and to give the Maltese Islands a viable degree of self-sufficiency.

101

6   INDUSTRY AND LIVELIHOOD

MANY of the obstacles in the way of creating suitable industries for the Maltese Islands are the same today as they were in the nineteenth century. The islands' natural resources have not changed. Their main raw material is limestone, and this is still used for most of the new building. The coralline and globigerina limestones, however, do not allow very deep or fertile soil on the main island of Malta. The blue clay on Gozo makes this the most fertile island of the group.

With such soils and a limited rainfall, irrigation is of prime importance. There are no rivers or natural lakes and most of the water has to be pumped from underground. There are two levels of aquifers: the mean sea-level aquifer and the perched aquifer; as their names suggest, the first is a layer of water held by the rock strata at sea level, and the second is a layer held by impervious clay above sea level. But these resources are no longer adequate and, to satisfy growing demands, the costly process of sea water distillation has become necessary.

On the other hand, Malta has excellent natural harbours, a versatile labour force and a good central position in the Mediterranean. The islands lie within easy reach of many important ports, including those in some of the developing North African countries, and they are on the route to the Suez Canal.

AGRICULTURE AND FISHING

Agriculture stands out as one of the industries most obviously hampered by the limitations of Maltese resources and traditions. Besides the water problem, there is the lack of large land-units. The pattern of small fields, terraced or enclosed by walls or hedges,

102

remains much as it has been for centuries. Only one-eighth of the holdings are over fifteen acres and few have irrigation systems. Working these small units are at least 7,000 full-time farmers and many more who work part-time supplementing another job. The total number engaged in agriculture, full and part-time, is about one-sixth of the employed population. It is clear that reforms needing the co-operation of such a large number of people are not easy to achieve.

Another obstacle to reform is the persisting use of old-fashioned farming methods. Maltese farmers, unaccustomed to producing high-quality goods for sophisticated markets, have been slow to adopt new techniques. In addition to grants and low-interest loans, government advisory services and publicity for more intensive methods are helping to combat the conservatism of farming communities. Diversification is also being encouraged, with an eye partly on export markets.

Until recently most of the agricultural produce was consumed locally, the main crops being potatoes, onions, melons, pumpkins, tomatoes, grapes and cereals. The export drive began with potatoes and dried onions and extended later to horticultural and glasshouse produce, including tomatoes, which attract especially high prices out of season, cut flowers, bulbs and seeds. Cattle, goats, pigs, poultry and rabbits are among the types of livestock bred in the islands today, with the emphasis on animals that can do without large spaces in which to graze or forage for food. For this reason, and because they yield products suitable for export, poultry farming and pig breeding have prospered.

The Department of Agriculture has an experimental farm on the main island and a livestock centre in Gozo. The state-owned Milk Marketing Undertaking aims to satisfy more of the local demand for milk and to decrease expenditure on imported tinned milk. It has been highly successful; milk yields have been rising and the production of cream, yoghourt, ricotta and soft cheeses has been increased.

103

Fishermen, like farmers, are not easily converted to new techniques. It seems wrong that these Mediterranean islands, within reach of so many varieties of edible fish, should have to import large quantites of fish each year. For centuries Maltese fishermen have worked the bays and inshore waters around the islands, catching *lampuki* and *fanfri* (pilotfish) in the autumn, and mackerel, bogue and scad during May, June and July. But the stocks of fish in these coastal waters have been depleted by overfishing. In order to expand the industry, larger and stronger boats, with the equipment for trawling or long-line fishing at greater distances from their home ports, are essential. Grants have been made by the government to assist this development, to increase the number of licensed motor-driven fishing vessels and to encourage Maltese fishermen to adapt their methods to their islands' needs.

WINES

One interesting branch of Maltese agriculture, with a unique history, is viticulture. Wine-making was introduced by the Phoenicians who brought the vine to Malta, calling it *dielja* which means the 'shade-maker'. The first vines grown for wine-making were planted in the hilly western districts near the more modern Qormi and Zabbar, and to this day the vineyards in this area produce the best wine.

The industry has fluctuated greatly throughout Maltese history. During the Middle Ages the population declined and vine-growing almost ceased. It was revived in the time of the Knights who decided that the Insola grape was the one best suited to the soil and climate of Malta, and this to a large extent remains the case. But in Gozo the tradition of farmer-priests, with their contacts in the Church overseas, led to the introduction of French grapes. Today more than half the vines in Gozo are of French origin.

Another lapse occurred in the eighteenth century when the

American War of Independence brought such great opportunities to Malta's cotton trade that most of the vineyards were converted into cotton plantations. Wine-growing was re-introduced about 1870 and continued in a desultory fashion during the next seventy years, but most of the wine consumed in the islands in this period was imported and the industry failed to expand. After 1939, the vineyards were used to grow vital wartime food and it was only when the fighting was over that the wine industry began to flourish. Although the Maltese drink somewhat less wine today than previously, due to the introduction of beer and soft drinks, there has been a substantial increase in local production, and more Maltese wine is being exported each year to Italy and Britain.

One unusual feature of the wine industry in Malta is the way in which the grapes are distributed and processed. The vineyards, owned by the government, the Church or hereditary landlords, are quite separate from the firms which process the wine. These firms send their brokers round the vineyards to assess the standard of the grapes and to recommend suitable types and quantities to their employers. There is no question of bargaining as, since 1965, the government has fixed the price per ton of grapes.

The vintage takes place in September and the grapes are then delivered to the factories. Except for the red wines which are fermented on the skin, and the comparatively small quantity of wine required by the Church, no fermentation occurs until October when the heat and humidity in the islands have decreased. Even with the modern equipment used by some of the bigger firms, where the processing is controlled in steel glass-lined vats, fermentation is not feasible before this time. Sulphur dioxide is used to arrest premature fermentation. The altar wine, which ferments naturally and is very pure indeed, is without doubt the finest wine. The largest factories use cultured yeast imported from Italy but some small firms use home grown yeast.

The chief vine grown, Insola, serves either for wine or else as a table grape, although not perfect for either. Improvements in the wine industry depend upon the introduction of a wider variety of grapes. Attempts to produce a sherry wine have been unsuccessful. Increasing exports of wine, however, reflect the growing popularity of Maltese wines and show the potential of this industry.

MODERN MANUFACTURE

The manufacturing industries have been those most exposed to innovation since the first five-year development plan began to take effect in 1959. Diversification and expansion have been the key-notes, and new ventures have been strongly encouraged. But there have been many problems. The Robens report of 1967 gave three basic obstacles to expansion, particularly in the smaller manufacturing firms : lack of factory and storage facilities, insufficient capital and inflexibility of managements in the traditional family units. As in agriculture, the conservative attitudes in family-owned businesses, and severe space limitations, have hindered expansion and development.

Among the old-established industries, the production of textiles has retained its position as one of the leading branches of Maltese industry. During the sixties, twelve new factories came into being to produce fabrics from natural and synthetic fibres both for export and the home market. In the export field the textile industry has had considerable success. In the mid-sixties, out of a total of £4.5 million earned in one year by manufactured exports, half was due to textiles, clothing and yarns.

But there is growing competition from Asian countries in the production of pure textiles and Malta faces the need to export more and more of its fabrics made up into clothing. Most exports in the past went to the United Kingdom and Italy but wider prospects have opened up for clothing (as for other manufactured goods) in North Africa and the Middle East. Meanwhile the

106

Page 107 : (*above*) Yacht marina; (*below*) beach scene.

Page 108: Gozitan hamlet.

demand in the Maltese Islands for ready-made clothes is increasing with the rise in standards of living, and this demand could be satisfied to a greater extent by local manufacture. This industry has great scope and although, by employing predominantly female labour, it is not likely to work miracles for the male unemployment problem, it is an indispensable asset to the Maltese economy.

The manufacture of furniture in metal and wood has made progress and some furniture is exported. But the industry lacks cohesion and factories large enough for the layout of modern production lines. There are increasing opportunities for exporting furniture for homes, offices and schools in less developed countries. Such openings exist also for metal fittings, containers and general household and office hardware. Many products of this type are profitable; they do not need complex factory installations and they are fairly easy to ship.

For much the same reasons, light precision engineering and the production of detergents, plastic packaging materials, shoes and leather goods find favour. There is a flourishing brewing and soft drinks industry, and scope exists for the manufacture of various chemicals if the water and power supplies can meet the demand of this activity. While a lack of suitable resources inhibits paper production, the Maltese have developed a profitable industry in printing. Costs are at present low enough to attract orders from overseas, even from countries as distant as the USA. In spite of the failure of the Rambler car-assembly plant mentioned in the previous chapter, this industry has been re-established on new lines, has proved successful, and some cars assembled in Malta are being exported. Buses are also being assembled in Malta. In general, the official priority is for new light industries which employ male workers, have a low content of expensive imported materials and promise well in accessible export markets.

If traditional Maltese handicrafts are nowadays less prominent in the industrial scene, they remain a distinctive feature and are unlikely to be driven into obscurity. The growing tourist trade provides a new incentive.

The craft with the longest tradition in the islands is pottery. In the museum in Valletta, cases of vases and urns with simple linear patterns testify to the skill of the inhabitants twenty centuries BC. The local clay, which fires to a beautiful terracotta, has provided the material for an enduring craft. More recently, a pottery was founded which produces glazed ware, thereby mixing the local clay with a stronger imported variety, adding impetus to a ceramic tradition going back some four thousand years.

Handweaving is a craft at which the Maltese excelled in the era of sailing ships when the islanders' sailcloth was renowned throughout the Mediterranean. The spinning and weaving of the cotton was done with wooden machinery turned by hand or by donkey. This industry ceased with the advent of steam ships but the Maltese had also spun the yarn and woven the cloth for their own clothes and this branch of the craft survives. Handwoven cloths with multicoloured patterns are produced today under the supervision of a company which influences design and maintains standards.

Maltese lace is famous and may be traced back to about 1640 when it was made mainly for the churches. After a lapse, the craft was resumed in the early nineteenth century, lace makers being brought from Genoa to instruct the Maltese. Black and cream silk thread was mostly used until the introduction of Irish linen thread in 1932, when exports of lace soon rose. Lack of materials during the war years led to a decline in the craft; lace workers were reduced to unpicking stockings to get enough thread but this thread was too coarse and the art was partially lost. Tourism has brought a revival and the craft continues as a cottage industry, mainly in Gozo.

Metalwork by hand is another traditional craft. The work is done in wrought iron, brass and precious metals, wrought iron being used for a type of balcony which abounds in Malta, and for gates, tables and lamps. The brass foundry, having produced articles for the churches for many years, now caters for a wider market, its speciality being the dolphin door-knockers which are a feature of Maltese houses. Gold and silver filigree work is a popular craft and the delicate jewellery which results is of a high standard.

Finally, there is a certain amount of handwork in specially imported wood, the best known product in this material being the Maltese briar pipe. The scarcity of indigenous wood is a limiting factor but good use is made of local bamboo and reeds in the manufacture of light furniture.

Maltese handicrafts are varied and of excellent quality, resting on traditions which reach far into the islands' past. As most of the crafts have been rejuvenated by the advent of mass tourism, the modern visitor is clearly helping to preserve an important facet of Maltese history.

THE CONSTRUCTION INDUSTRY

The inexhaustible supply of Maltese limestone, which carves easily and weathers well, has encouraged a long tradition of skill and craftsmanship in the building trade. Maltese architecture (which is considered in the next chapter) and construction technique have been influenced strongly by the abundance of stone and the shortage of wood.

The post-war boom in construction work having levelled out by the end of the 1950s, the introduction of new projects and industries to the islands with the first plans for diversification, instilled fresh life into the industry and, by the mid-sixties, over one-tenth of the employed population were working in quarrying and construction. Demands for new roads, bridges, warehouses, factories, flats and hotels increased with the growing commercial activity and the influx of foreign tourists, and new schools, colleges and public buildings were needed to keep education and public services in line with the country's overall development. This trend has led to the expansion of ancillary services and these, in turn, have brought more work to the construction industry; among others, the gas, electricity, telephone, water and sewerage authorities have been important sources of new building contracts.

More recently, the construction industry has had difficulty in meeting all its orders. This applies both to the provision of hotels, villas and flats for visitors and also to the supply of housing for the Maltese whose demands have increased with the rising standards of living. Building programmes have been held up, mainly by shortage of skilled workers, and there has been pressure on the government to allow more scope for foreign contractors eager to establish themselves in Malta.

PASSENGER TRANSPORT

In the mid-nineteenth century, apart from small coastal vessels, there were two main forms of local public transport. The *dghajsa*, a long-established cousin to the Venetian gondola, carried people across the Maltese creeks, and these brightly painted boats can still be seen in the harbours around Valletta. The *karrozzin*, or horse-drawn cab, became a feature of the Maltese scene in 1856, being first known as a 'victoria' after the British queen.

The first step towards more modern transportation was a railway, built and run by a British company with second-hand engines and rolling stock from the Isle of Wight. The official opening day in 1883 saw the first engine, hauling eight carriages

decorated with flags and palms, leave Valletta for Mdina. In
England the early trains had been called 'iron horses' but the
Maltese aptly named theirs *il-vapur tal-art*, meaning 'land-
steamer'. The journey of twelve kilometres lasted twenty-five
minutes, with stops at Hamrun, Birkirkara, Attard and Rabat

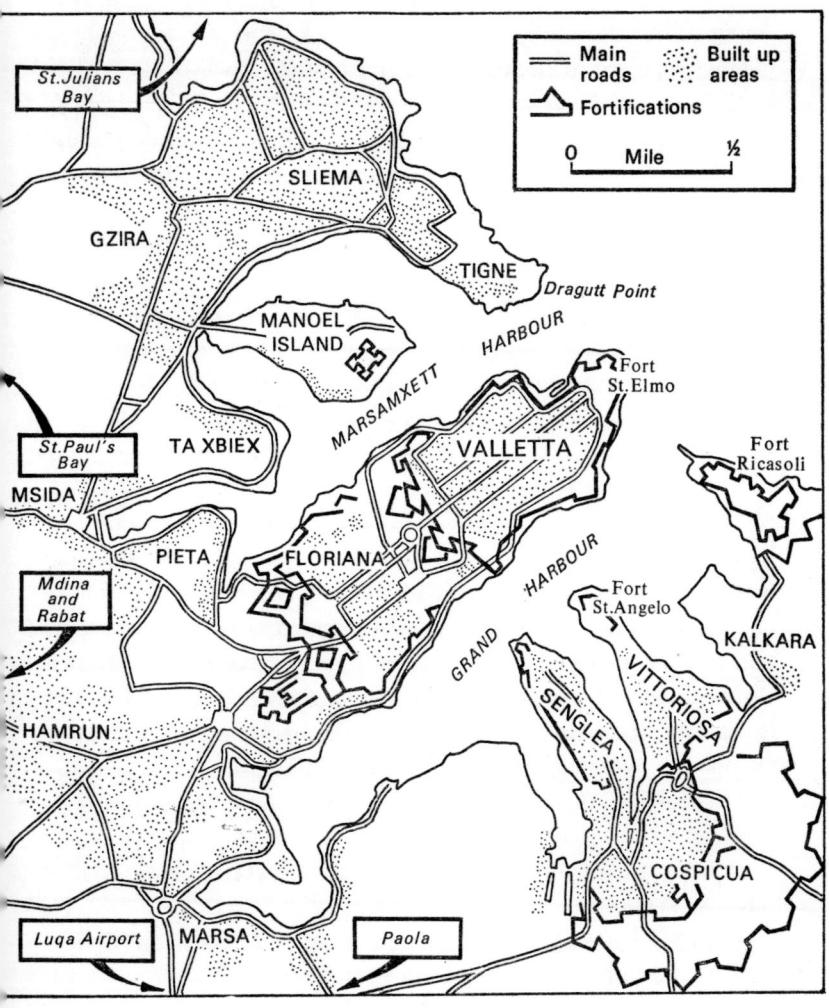

(the station for Mdina), and optional halts at Floriana, San Anton and Wied Incita. Tickets from Valletta to Rabat cost 7d first class and 3½d third class. The trains were very popular at first and the company took £50-£60 each day, but by 1890 their daily income had sunk to £13; the company lost £80,000 over a seven-year period and the old engines became badly in need of repair. The Maltese government took over the railway, had the engines repaired at the dockyard and built a tunnel below Mdina to the new army barracks at Mtarfa. In 1892 the trains began to flourish again and a plan was made to construct an underground station beneath Valletta, with an entrance near the market place, but this was never realised.

The track, much of it single, ran through open country for most of the journey, with two tunnels, each less than a mile in length. The stations tended to be on the outskirts of the towns. In Valletta, passengers had to make for the edge of the city and walk down a tunnelled incline to the platform which was built on arches in the main ditch below the city walls; the remains of this platform are visible today from the bridge linking Kingsgate to Floriana. The station in Floriana, near the Argotti Gardens, was underground. Birkirkara had a particularly fine station overlooked by the steeple of a ruined church. The stage from Attard to Rabat was the longest, and the station at Rabat was at the bottom of a wide cutting a hundred feet below the town itself. Passengers had to walk up an incline or a steep flight of stairs to the Siggiewi-Rabat road, and thence up the rough slopes to the town. The route from the terminus at Mtarfa to the barracks was even more exhausting, with an uphill walk of three-quarters of a mile.

The railway ran until April 1931. The stations have since been demolished or converted to other uses and the old tracks are overgrown. A few of the railway carriages survive, being used as bus-stop shelters.

The Maltese electric tram system enjoyed an even briefer heyday. At one time there were three routes from the Valletta terminus at Kingsgate: to Hamrun and Birkirkara, to Qormi and Zebbug, and to Paola and Cospicua. The trams ran at five-minute intervals and stopped at the wish of passengers; a ticket for any distance cost 2d. The service was opened in 1905, dying a natural death after the First World War with the increasing use of motor-powered vehicles.

Today it is the buses that hold the monopoly of the inland passenger transport system. The bus companies are privately owned but are not strictly competitive as each company usually serves one particular district. The routes are not numbered, each having a distinctive colour for its buses and stop signs. The termi-nuses are at Kingsgate, just outside Valletta, and at Castile Place which is within the city walls. Most of the routes follow the main roads which fan out from the capital across the island. There are about six hundred buses and the services are profitable. It is said that, in addition to the small, official fee payable to the police, black market payments of over £1,000 have been made in the past to companies relinquishing their licence.

Water transport across the harbours and between the islands is surprisingly sparse. There is a ferry, for passengers, cars, light cargoes and mails, from the coast north-west of the Marfa Ridge to Mgarr in Gozo, and a hydrofoil links Valletta with the islands of Comino and Gozo. Until recently there were regular ferries across Grand Harbour and between Sliema and Valletta, saving lengthy journeys along the congested roads which meander around the harbour creeks, but the vessels were old-fashioned and became uneconomic. Apart from the time saved, a ride in these ferries showed the grandeur of Valletta and the sparkling beauty of the creeks to best advantage. With new equipment, the Sliema-Val-letta ferry in particular could be a paying proposition; a con-venience for the commuter and an attraction for the tourist.

There is an adequate supply of taxis, self-drive cars and yachts for hire. The number of vehicles crowding the islands' six hundred miles of road has been increasing at an alarming rate and severe

115

traffic jams occur at peak hours. The towns, with their narrow streets, are unsuited to heavy traffic. The threat to the pedestrian, as to urban amenity in general, is becoming serious. This is notably the case in Valletta despite the ruling that drivers must hold a special licence to enter the city; although traffic is banned in Kingsway in the evenings so that the Maltese can stroll unmolested in the street, this is a small dam against the growing torrent. By failing to develop an intelligent public transport system on land and water, the Maltese government, its compact islands cut off by the sea from continental road systems, has missed a golden opportunity to limit car ownership and to preserve its country as a relatively traffic-free sanctuary.

THE MALTESE DOCKS

The docks have long been of fundamental importance to the Maltese economy and, until recently the largest single industrial employer, were supported by a steady income from the British services. In the palmy days when profit was not a consideration, the docks were not run in the most economic fashion; during much of the year, when the fleet was cruising, the work could hardly be called arduous. When the run-down of the services began in the late fifties, the docks soon found themselves critically over-manned and under-employed. A radical plan was needed to attract civilian ship-repairing contracts in competition with other yards in the Mediterranean, and to re-organise with this new kind of customer in view.

The first step was to offer a 99-year lease, with development grants, to any suitable firm willing to take over the management of the docks. The task promised to be risky and difficult and there was no rush of applicants. In 1959, however, C. H. Bailey & Co Ltd of South Wales agreed to form a company in Malta with the promise of a £7.5 million grant to help with conversion costs. A

116

deep water quay, transit sheds, a grain silo and new mechanical handling equipment increased the docks' facilities considerably but the best use was not made of these and the docks continued to lose money. The uncertainty of the situation and the fear of redundancy among the workers increased labour problems. Within four years, after disagreements between Bailey and the authorities, the company withdrew.

There are more than thirty registered trade unions for employees in Malta, the largest and strongest being the General Workers Union to which the dockers belong. This union has over 15,000 more members than any other union, strong sympathies with the Maltese labour party and a distinctly militant tradition. One of the chief difficulties, besides the insecurity felt by the dockers, was that of achieving a balanced wages policy. While wages need to move upward with the rising standard of living, they must be kept low enough to ensure that the Maltese docks are not priced out of the market. Rationalisation has helped to keep costs down but it led to the redundancy of more than 1,000 dockworkers in the mid-sixties, reducing the numbers employed to about 4,000. This process, straining relations between management and the union, has impeded the drive for greater efficiency.

In 1964 the Swan Hunter Group Ltd replaced Bailey as managing agents of the docks. No 4 dock was enlarged to take 100,000-ton ships, the yacht repair yard at Manoel Island was extended to cope with vessels up to 200 feet in length, and the tanker-cleaning installation at Ricasoli was completed. As the necessary changes from a naval to a commercial function gained momentum, the turnover of the docks increased by nearly one-third in the first three years under the new management. Further measures have included improvements to general port facilities, an increase in wharfage area and, to make best use of inherited plant and equipment, a deliberate move towards greater diversification.

TOURISM

In recent years, tourism has become the Maltese Islands' fastest-growing industry and a prime source of revenue and livelihood. In the early sixties, the annual number of visitors to Malta could be counted in five figures; during this decade they multiplied eight-fold, to be measured in six figures. The majority of tourists are still from Britain, reflecting both sentiment and the more practical language and currency advantages. As tourist facilities expand and new direct air-links are forged, visitors are gradually being sought from further afield. The quality and accuracy of Maltese tourist publicity is of a commendably high standard.

Climate, character and amenity give the islands the bonus of a virtually year-round season. While facilities for tourists have been greatly improved and generally compare well with those of other Mediterranean countries, shortage of space—particularly, shortage of sandy beaches—is a serious limiting factor. Amends have been made by developing and emphasising distinctive attractions. One among several examples is the superb yachting centre in Marsamxett Harbour. At its quays, yachts can be supplied with water, electricity, telephone and radio, and there are ample facilities for refuelling, provisioning, repairs and caretaking. A club, shopping and car parking complex on Manoel Island is part of the plan. Other visitors enjoy the islands because of their easily-accessible wealth of beautiful architecture and historic remains. Monuments are restored and preserved with devoted care; the National Museum, too, has lately been extended and improved.

Apart from the space problem, the further growth of tourism has been hindered by three factors : shortage of capacity in the construction industry, civil service inertia (for example, in the granting of permits and licenses) and hesitant government policy (for example, in deciding the extent to which the islands should cater for the popular 'package tour' market). But making haste slowly with tourism can have its advantages : national integrity

118

and the landscape may escape defilement. Fortunately, this has been the case so far in the Maltese Islands.

IMPORTS AND EXPORTS

The value of the islands' imports rose steadily from under £30 million in the late fifties to over £40 million in the late sixties. This increase was due both to higher demands for consumer goods, and to the needs of expanding industries for capital equipment, raw materials and semi-manufactured goods. In their turn, exports (including re-exports, particularly in the form of fuel and supplies to ships and aircraft) more than doubled in value in the same period, rising from about £4 million to well over £10 million. The net result, despite the healthy export trade, was a worsening of the trade deficit by £5 million or so to around £30 million. As the new industries get into their stride, boosting export figures while helping also to satisfy home demands, the burden of the trade gap should be lightened.

The largest share of imports have come traditionally from the UK, the next biggest supplier being Italy. The direction of trade is now gradually changing. Exports, formerly to a critical extent to the UK, are penetrating beyond the EFTA countries to other European markets and to neighbouring markets in North Africa; there are good prospects also in the Levant and further afield on the African continent, and these are not being neglected.

The annual Malta Trade Fair, established in 1951, is a focal point of growing importance in Maltese trade. Managed by a government-sponsored corporation, the fair caters for both foreign and Maltese exhibitors. Besides supporting their native exhibition, Maltese industries are appearing increasingly in similar ventures abroad, notably in Italian, Libyan and other neighbouring trade fairs.

Less helpful to Maltese trade are some of the delays and costs

119

involved in freight shipment. For example, as the exporting season for perishable goods such as fruit and flowers does not coincide with the peak months for passenger flights, the provision of extra air services remains uneconomic until profitable two-way loads can be generated by extra complimentary traffic. Shipment by sea has long been a cause of frustration. Vessels of various nationalities take on cargo from Malta, but their calls may be irregular and carriage may be delayed by diverse routing or by long waits for cargo in other ports on the way. With the volume of trade rising and the new free port in view, shipment facilities will no doubt improve. Meanwhile, for a country seeking to compete in export markets, any incapacity to quote prompt or punctual delivery dates can be crucial.

WELFARE AND EDUCATION

Government service provides employment for about 18,000 islanders or one-fifth of the working population. On the whole, the official machine has acquitted itself well during the period of change and adjustment following the attainment of independence. Among the departments which have grappled successfully with new tasks and problems, are those concerned with trade and industry, with education and health, and with the social services in general.

The Department of Social Services, formed in 1965 with seventeen area-offices in Malta and two in Gozo, administers the national insurance scheme whereby coverage has been extended to practically the entire population of Malta, whether employed, self-employed or unemployed. The national assistance programme renders social assistance in cases of sickness, leprosy and tuberculosis and, subject to a means test, covers institutional relief payments and general grants for medical aid. The welfare service carries out social work among families and runs homes and approved schools for girls and boys.

Government welfare, health and education schemes run side-by-side with extensive facilities provided by the Church authorities and lay sponsors. In general, the Maltese are a healthy race. The state medical service is efficient and includes free specialist and hospital treatment; there is a district nurse service, and the hospitals, of which nine are government-subsidised and four are private, provide over 4,000 beds.

Education, compulsory for all children between the ages of six and fourteen, is a fast-expanding service. Government expenditure exceeded £2 million a year in the mid-sixties compared with less than £1 million ten years before. There are over a hundred infants' and primary schools; at least six grammar and four secondary technical schools; special schools for handicapped children; and continuation courses at a technical institute for boys of fourteen to seventeen years of age.

Apprenticeships may be served in industry by any boy over the age of fourteen who reaches a certain standard of education and shows an aptitude for his chosen trade. A contract for about five years is signed by the apprentice, his parents and his employer. The government subsidises the employer for the first few years of each apprenticeship and the boy receives a small wage. Apprentices at the drydocks attend the Dockyard Technical College for theoretical training; all other apprentices attend an apprenticeship school run by the Department of Education. The recently completed College of Arts, Science and Technology provides higher technological training, including advanced courses in science, business, economics, art, textiles and catering. There are also two teachers' training colleges.

The Royal University of Malta began as a Jesuit college in 1592 with papal authority to confer degrees in philosophy and theology. It gained full university status in 1769. Today, two centuries later, it has re-established itself on a fine new site on high ground above Msida, degrees being conferred in theology, medicine, law, various branches of the arts and science, and other subjects. Former two-year courses have been extended to three years; there are about a thousand students and annual expenditure on this impressive university now approaches £500,000.

PASSING THE WORD

Any appraisal of Maltese journalism and broadcasting serves as a reminder that this small island-group contains a polyglot people of diverse tastes and cultures. There are at least half-a-dozen daily newspapers, some three each in English and Maltese, and there are regular broadcasting channels in both languages.

The Broadcasting Authority, an independent statutory body receiving its income from licence fees, is responsible for all broadcasting in the islands, but most of the programmes are provided by commercial companies : Rediffusion (Malta) Ltd for sound broadcasting, and the Malta Television Service Ltd for television. The Rediffusion company broadcasts on two channels, one in Maltese and the other in English, with an increasing proportion of locally-produced programmes, augmented by relays from the BBC. Malta Television, likewise, is expanding local programme production to satisfy calls for longer broadcasting hours and greater variety; by the mid-sixties there was already one television set for every eight inhabitants.

Educational broadcasting on television is a recent development which started in 1966 with two programmes for schools, on physics and the English language. Educational programmes on radio cover a wide syllabus for children and adults, provision for the latter ranging from 'Parliamentary Procedure and Constitutional Practice' to interviews with leading poets from Malta and Gozo.

The Maltese telephone and postal services are based closely on the British model—even the red pillar boxes are the same. The

Maltese produce beautifully-designed stamps, popular with phila-
telists all over the world. As in other countries, the telephone
service, with its network of automatic exchanges, is struggling to
keep pace with rapidly-increasing demand; as befits a modern
trading nation, the existing cable services to parts of Europe,
Africa and North America are being extended.

OTHER WORK—AND NONE

Commerce and personal services provide a livelihood for at least
20,000 Maltese, many of them the owners or employees of small
family businesses. This sector of the community—importers,
brokers, shopkeepers, caterers, hauliers, home helps, people working in banks, bars and barber shops—have been making good
money with the growth of tourism and domestic prosperity. In
general, the pattern of employment is undergoing a fairly drastic
process of change spread over a twenty-year period. Until recently,
the creation of new jobs having failed to keep pace with redun-
dancies and unemployment, the process has not been painless. At
one point in the mid-sixties, the unemployment figure rose to 10
per cent of the working population.

For many years emigration has been recognised as one solution
to the unemployment problem. In 1964, the peak year of the
sixties, the emigrant total reached almost 9,000, but within two
years this figure had eased back to less than half. The government, besides subsidising emigrants' fares, has an agreement with
Australia to help provide capital for those hoping to start a new
life in that country. Traditionally, the bulk of Maltese emigrants
make their way to Australia; indeed, over 100,000 Maltese
(equivalent to one in three of the islands' population) now live
there, supporting a newspaper in their own language—an impressive 'colonising' effort! Britain, Canada and the USA, in that order,
are the most favoured destinations after Australia.

123

Island races make great travellers and, even at the best of times, Maltese people will seek broader horizons beyond their own shores. When this is by choice rather than necessity, and when there is enough work in their own islands for all who seek it, the Maltese' own promised land will at last be in sight.

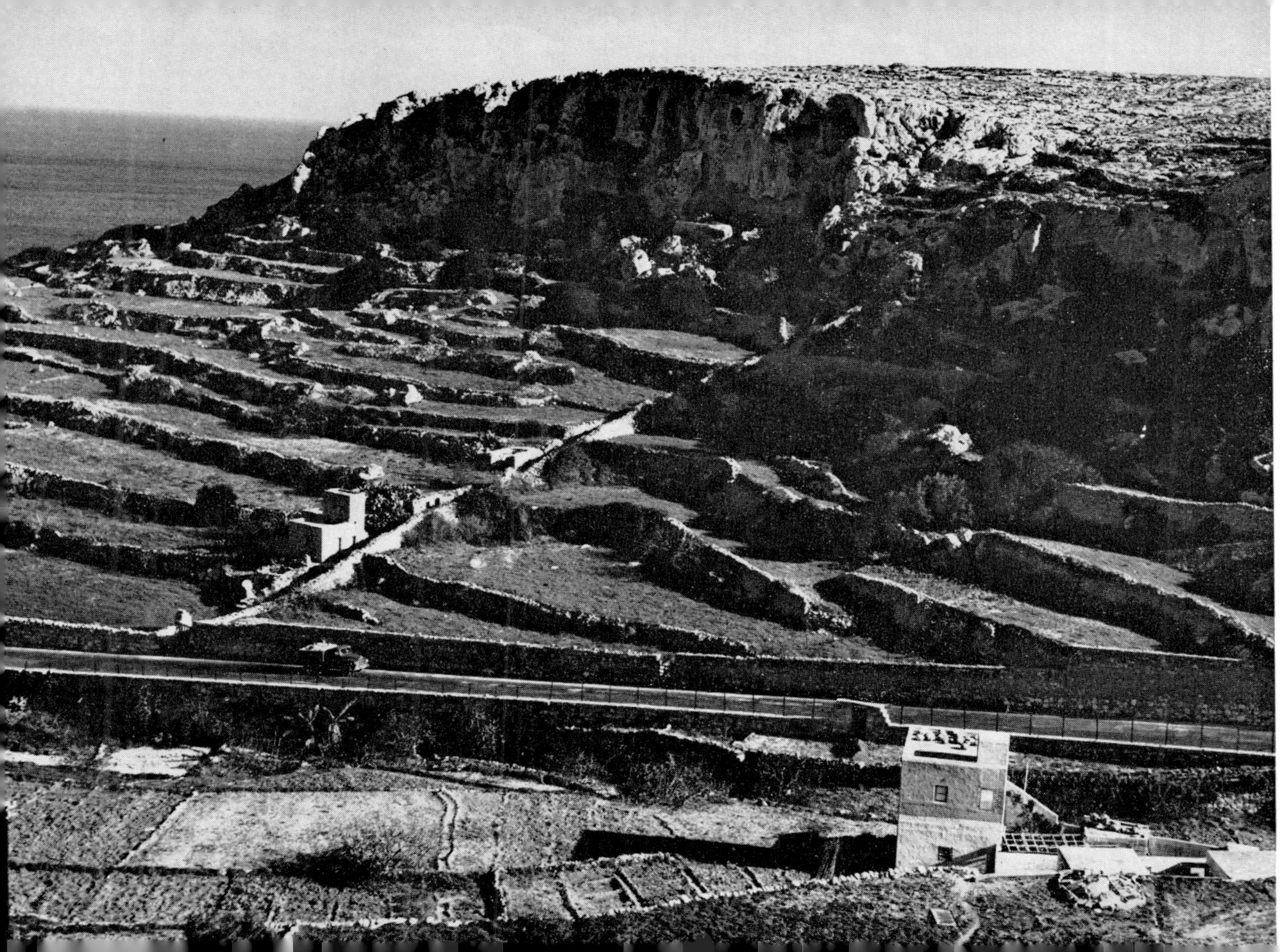

Page 125: Terraced countryside.

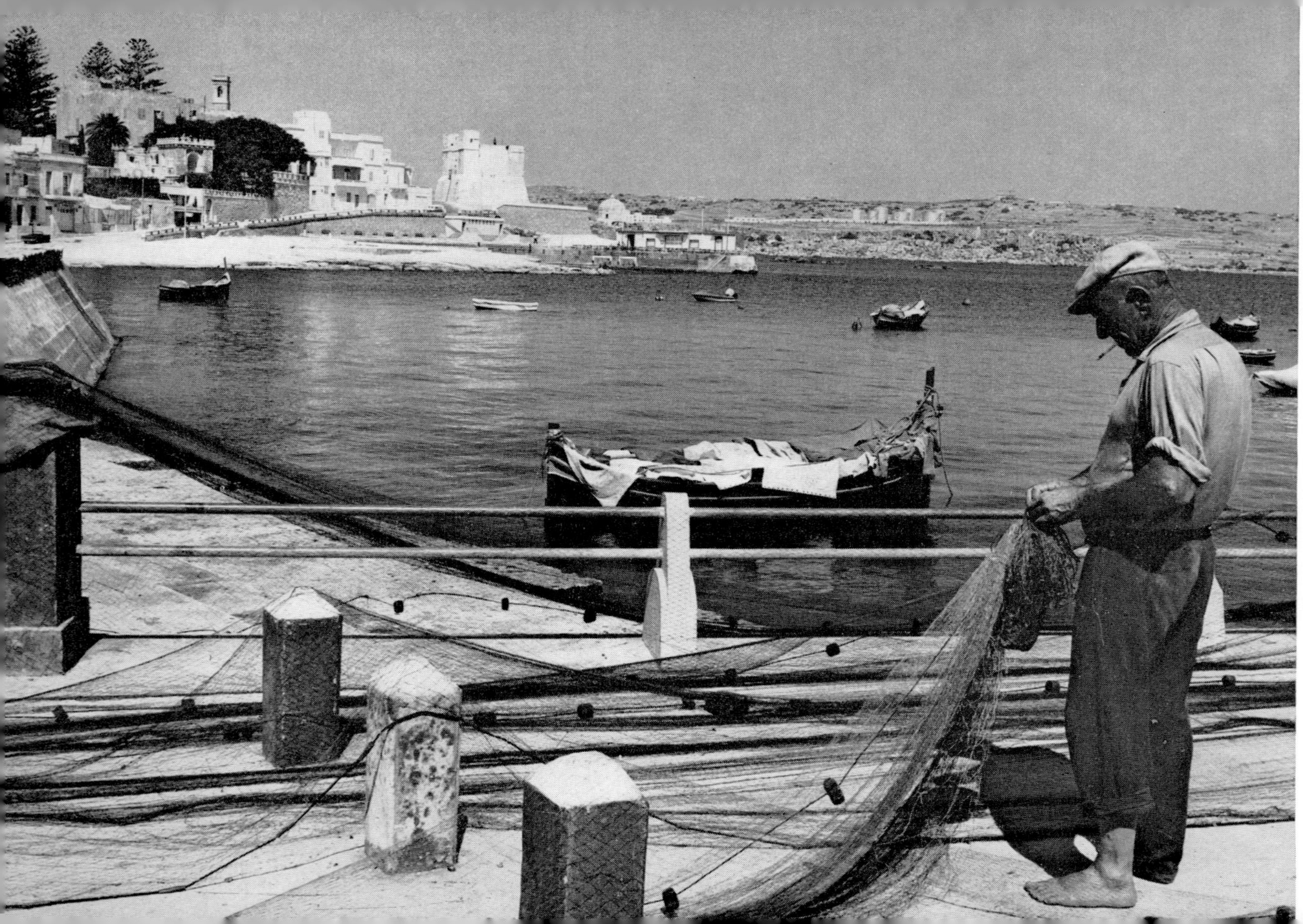

Page 126:
Fishing port.

7   ARTS AND ARCHITECTURE

ARCHITECTURE has always taken first place among the Maltese arts and, over the centuries, has been subject to three main influences: the islanders' religious faith, the self-aggrandisement of their rulers and the need for protection against invasion. These influences have created a wealth of temples, churches, palaces, mansions and fortresses which to-day form one of the finest collections of architecture in the world.

The Knights of St John, who continued the tradition of distinctive military architecture, were the chief patrons of style and opulence in urban buildings, but the Church, before, during and after their time growing steadily in power and affluence, has long been a prime source of encouragement of the arts and, in particular, the chief initiator of religious architecture. An important impetus has been rivalry between parishes, each community desiring a bigger or better church, with richer decorations, or more paintings and frescoes, or finer sculptures, than the village down the road. Besides architecture, therefore, painting and sculpture have flourished, thanks both to priestly fervour and to layman's toil and self-denial; the bishops have always insisted that the villagers' own coin and muscle must do their bit.

The arts of literature, drama and poetry have been hampered by problems of language and, although the flow of published material in the Maltese tongue is growing, there is a lack of significant tradition. Music has been a part of the Maltese way of life for centuries; music for festivals, marches for processions, hymns for ceremonies and folk songs for relaxation. Here again, however, few famous names stand out, whether of composers or

H

musicians; music, chiefly a communal art, has been taken too much for granted.

While the traditions of painting and sculpture in Malta by no means compare with those of architecture, they cannot be overlooked. During the seventeenth century three great Italian masters came to work in Malta : Michelangelo Merisi da Caravaggio, Filippo Paladini and Mattia Preti. Caravaggio's two most famous paintings in Malta, *St Jerome* and the *Beheading of St John*, hang in St John's Co-Cathedral in Valletta. Preti painted the ceiling of this cathedral with scenes from the life of St John—one of his finest and most exacting works. Besides this, a painting of his may be found in nearly every Maltese town and village. All three men were a strong influence on Maltese painters in later centuries.

During the eighteenth century two names are prominent in Maltese art : Francesco Zahra and Antoine de Favray. Although French by birth, Favray lived in Malta for over twenty years, producing many fine altarpieces, religious paintings, portraits and landscapes. The most powerful painter in the nineteenth century was undoubtedly Guiseppe Cali. *St Jerome* in the Church of the Sacred Heart, Sliema, a fine example of his early work, is thought by many to be his masterpiece; the large altarpieces and paintings on the ceiling of St Dominic's, Valletta, are his; while *The Glory of St Francis* in St Francis' Church, Valletta, shows us the quality of his late period. Examples of this painter's work are to be seen everywhere, over six hundred of his works being listed for Malta alone.

Sculpture claims a longer tradition than painting, having played its part in some of the neolithic civilisations. The oldest examples of Maltese sculpture are terracotta statuettes and limestone figures dating from over 1,000 years BC. Their style is remarkable; unlike the pottery of the early settlers, which is delicately made with linear designs, these figures are gross and ugly. Some are female and some asexual, with thick, foreshortened limbs and vast,

128

grotesque bodies. They are skilfully executed, nevertheless, and the physical distortions cannot be dismissed as clumsy craftsmanship. It is thought their grossness may have symbolised fertility or conveyed ideas of power and protection in some cult of which little is known.

Nearer modern times, Maltese-born Melchiorre Gafa stands out as a sculptor of exceptional talent. In the present century, Antonio Sciortino, who died in 1947, is undoubtedly the great name in sculpture, his work having won international praise. At first, he was strongly influenced by Rodin and Meunier; later, he became fascinated by the representation of speed and movement in static material. His monument to the Great Siege of 1565 can be seen in Kingsway, and many of his busts and statuettes are to be found in the gardens of Valletta and Floriana. His pupil, Vincent Apap, has done notable work and so has another contemporary sculptor, Carlo Pisi.

EARLY ARCHITECTURE

Maltese architecture has a tradition even older than that of sculpture, the stone temples built by some of the earliest settlers dating back beyond reach of the written word and almost beyond the imagination. The prehistoric people who created these temples were probably troglodyte, living in houses carved out of the solid rock. When they emerged above ground, it is more than likely that they used tents, at first shaped like a cone and then built on the ridge-tent pattern with semi-circular ends.

Both types of dwelling had their influence on later building techniques in Malta. Troglodyte building has continued for centuries in differing forms: catacombs were carved out of the limestone by the Christians in the fourth and fifth centuries, and the church in Fort St Angelo was built underground in the eleventh century. During the next several hundred years, networks of passages were burrowed under the fortifications, and more recently, caves and shelters were cut into the rock to give protection from the hazards of the Second World War. From the ridge-tent comes the basic design of many medieval palaces in Malta, with their three interlocking rooms opening into each other without a corridor. The central room was a hall, with a door into the street at the front and another into the courtyard behind, while the smaller rooms at each end corresponded to the end sections of the prehistoric buildings. This pattern remained the same over many centuries.

Other important influences on the islands' architecture have been the lack of timber and the nature of Maltese limestone. The beams supporting the roofs of the early churches had to be of stone and, for technical (including safety) reasons, the stone beams were limited to six-foot lengths. So to give the churches sufficient width, and their roofs enough support, arches and piers were projected into the nave at six-foot intervals. The result was a series of chunky bays with a narrow nave between them. A further characteristic of these churches was dictated by the weather : the windows had to be the right size to keep the buildings cool in the summer and, in the winter, protect the occupants from biting winds.

The number of buildings worth describing fully is so large that only a small selection can be covered here. Six buildings have been chosen, all of which reveal something typical of Maltese architecture and yet are different enough in style, purpose and location to demonstrate the variety of architectural achievement in the islands. A photograph of each building appears in this book. It may be noted that the chosen buildings are not necessarily the greatest or finest pieces of architecture of their type but each can claim distinction as a blend of the traditional and the unique. Thus we have have a cathedral, a Gozitan church, an old country home, a fort, a theatre and an auberge.

MDINA CATHEDRAL

Mdina Cathedral is the focal point of Malta's former capital city and for centuries was also the focal point of the islands' religion. Since 1816 the Church of St John in Valletta has had the status of co-cathedral with equal rights and dignities, but it is in Mdina that the story of Maltese Christianity begins. The legend goes that the cathedral stands on the site of the house of the Roman governor Publius, whose father was cured by St Paul after the famous shipwreck. Publius himself was converted to Christianity and a Christian community slowly grew up which held its meetings in the governor's house. The first church was built there in the fourth century when the Edict of Milan ensured greater freedom from religious persecution, and it was dedicated to St Paul.

By the eleventh century the church, had fallen into decay and was restored and improved by Roger the Norman. A violent earthquake destroyed it in 1693, however, and the present building was begun four years later. The architect was Lorenzo Gafa (brother of the sculptor, Melchiorre Gafa) who had designed many churches in the islands, including fine parish churches in Zejtun and Vittoriosa, and the cathedral in Gozo. At this period he was at the height of his powers and his confidence can be sensed from the perfect proportions of the cathedral façade in Mdina, and his daring treatment of the dome.

When seen for the first time across St Paul's Square, the baroque façade givens an impression of balance and great dignity. The central section containing the west door is set slightly forward from the two adjacent side sections, each of which carries a low bell tower. The pilasters used on the façade are plain and these, together with large areas of undecorated stonework below the bell towers, emphasise the basic lines of the building. The dome is one of Gafa's masterpieces. It is enhanced at eight points by the addition of small pilasters, so that the drum more resembles an

131

octagon, and from each of these a large scroll curves up to the top of the dome.

The cathedral is built in the traditional shape of the Latin cross. Inside, the three aisle bays between the west door and the transepts are linked by intercommunicating arches, and each bay is lit by oval windows. The rounded apse, with its four marble pilasters, is the only section of the earlier church saved from the devastation of the earthquake.

The first impression of the cathedral's interior is one of richness. The pilasters are of marble in veined grey and red, the gilded carvings over the archways and on the capitals add to the splendour. The cathedral possesses a considerable amount of Maltese silver in the form of candlesticks and pendant lamps, even the edges of the high altar being of beaten silver. There are many carvings and paintings depicting the life of St Paul, notably the fresco in the apse of St Paul's shipwreck, and the altarpiece of his conversion, both by Mattia Preti. The fresco in the dome, of the glory of St Paul, has recently been re-done by Mario Caffaro Rore of Turin. There is a statue of Publius just inside the main entrance.

The cross behind the main altar is said to be the one carried into Jerusalem by Godfrey de Bouillon at the head of the crusaders. On either side of the main altar is a chapel; the Chapel of the Blessed Sacrament contains a revered painting of the Madonna, which is covered with silver and jewels and is popularly attributed to St Luke, but more likely dates from the thirteenth century. Also within this chapel are the tombs of past bishops, and their green hats hang from the archway over the chapel entrance. The Chapel of the Crucifix to the south of the main altar is less spectacular but contains a fine crucifix by Fra Innocenzo, a Franciscan monk. The sacristy doors are carved from Irish bog oak with a different design on each panel, and serve as a final reminder of the cathedral's turbulent history for they, like the apse, survived the earthquake of 1693, having once stood at the west entrance of the church built by Roger the Norman.

A CHURCH IN GOZO

The Church of St Peter and St Paul stands in the village of Nadur on the second highest hill in the island of Gozo, commanding fine views over the Maltese islands and the Mediterranean—the word *nadur* coming from an Arabic word meaning 'to see'. This church is a proud example of the achievements of local enthusiasm and determination translated into religious splendour though Nadur, as it happens, has the advantage that its parishioners are perhaps more prosperous than usual.

The people, like others in Gozo, are farmers and seafarers, but a high proportion of these own the houses they occupy, are landlords and employers and, in many cases, enjoy supplementary incomes as businessmen (some of whom commute to the main island) or in the form of remittances from relatives who have emigrated. Nature has helped by endowing Nadur with fertile land suited particularly to fruit-growing, but hard work and good management deserve much of the credit.

As might be expected, inter-parish rivalry plays a significant part in the life of Nadur. When the annual *festa* comes round, every penny and every ounce of energy the people can raise goes into the celebrations, partly to demonstrate to neighbouring parishes the superiority of their church and their saint, and partly just for fun. The celebrations at the church in Nadur are outstanding for their colour and richness. The walls of the church are hung with red tapestry and the clergy wear heavily embroidered vestments. Candlesticks of wrought silver flicker on the marble altars and the statues of the patron saints stand on pedestals of silver, intricately worked.

The effect is heightened by the magnificence of the church's interior. The altar rails and pillars are made of onyx from Iran

133

and Morocco; the stained glass windows are from France; the marble alone, covering much of the interior, cost £27,000, a sum collected in only three years by less than 4,000 parishioners. There is a painting of St Peter and St Paul by Preti, and several other paintings by the Maltese artist Lazarus Pizani.

The present church dates back to 1760; its architect was Guiseppe Bonnice, who designed also the Church of St Publius in Floriana and the impressive customs house in Valletta. When the church was blessed in 1804, it consisted only of the nave, the transepts and the chancel; the aisle, façades and dome were added later. The perfect equilibrium of the 100-foot high dome can be gauged by the fact that the original plaster has no sign of any crack.

The façade of the church is ornately splendid. Steps lead up to the west door between statues of the two titular saints, the door being flanked by coupled pillars and pilasters. The double windows in the side sections of the façade are unusual in that only one of each admits light, the others simply giving symmetry to the design. Above these windows are turrets surmounted by torches carved in stone; the two bell towers are set further back and jut out slightly on each side.

Above the pediment of the entrance rise three levels, supported by pilasters alternately fluted and plain, carrying a sculpture of Our Lady of the Rosary by Melchiorre Gafa, a clock and a final turret with a triple cross above it. Behind this rises the dome itself. In marked contrast to the square and balanced restraint of the cathedral in Mdina, the façade of this church is essentially triangular, rising to a single climax with the cross above the dome.

GOMERINO

Down a narrow winding lane not far from Rabat, the country house of Gomerino comes into view, half-hidden by trees on a hill overlooking the countryside from Dingli to Mdina. From its tall entrance gates, a rough and even narrower drive winds up through carob, almond and olive trees to the red façade of the one-storey building. At the approaches to the house are fruit trees of many kinds—pomegranate, citrus, peaches, pears and plums; and on the higher ground, succulent prickly-pear plants, with grapevines sprawling over the shallow, rubble-walled terraces. A spring which rises to the north of the house, besides supplying other districts by aqueduct, has made the grounds and the valley below the house one of the greener and more fertile areas on the island.

'Gomerino' is the Italian name for the house; to many Maltese it is known as *Ghemieri*. The 'gh' in this word is silent and possibly derives from the Arabic *emir*, and this accounts for the theory that the present house stands on the site of the residence of the Arabic ruler during the eleventh century. The Arabic cemetery lies not far from the grounds of the house.

Later the land became a Maltese fief, granted first to Guglielmo Surdo by Frederick, King of Sicily, and passed later from one feudal lord to another until, at the marriage of Beatrice Cassia to Paolo Testaferrata, it came into the Testaferrata family. In 1710 the Grand Master of the Knights conferred the title of Baron of Gomerino on Paolo Testaferrata. The present owner of the house, the Most Noble Baroness Testaferrata Abela, is the tenth member of the family to inherit the property.

The date when the present house was built is open to dispute. It seems likely that the existing main building was designed by an Italian architect, perhaps Carapecchio, in the eighteenth century. But the earliest parts of the house, the slave quarters and the kitchen, are clearly much older. The former slave quarters, to the left of the house, and the former stables and outhouses, are now occupied by tenants who work the land. Originally there were only two families, employed as retainers, who leased their own plots of land from the owners. But the families having since multiplied and split, the rooms in the old buildings have been partitioned and divided, while rented cottages hidden in the valley accommodate further labourers.

Thus, the house is the centre of an almost self-contained community. The children attend a small school on the site of what was the officers' mess when the army took over the property in the Second World War. The tenants worship in the chapel of the house, in which mass is celebrated every Sunday by a priest from Rabat.

This chapel, built onto the right side of the house, was dedicated to St Anthony the Abbot in 1718. It has a triangular coping stone surmounted by a stone cross which stands above the roof of the main building, providing a focal point to the architecture of the house. Apart from a bell tower, the main decoration outside is the heraldic coat of arms with a bull and three stars and the family motto : *non nisi per ardua*. The interior is austere by catholic standards. A marble plaque commemorating the chapel's dedication looks down on plain wooden benches; otherwise the only embellishments are the large, stone-framed oil paintings of the Immaculate Conception, St Anthony of Padua and St Philip Neri, above the altar.

Within the house itself there is a striking mixture of old and new. The kitchen contains a vast stone cooking range which originally had five apertures through which the flames from the fire heated the cooking pots. Since gas cooking was installed, four of these have been filled in with tiles and the fifth covered by an ancient brass boiler. The kitchen floor is of uneven flagstones and, overhead, huge stone beams are supported by arches. The walls are more than three feet thick.

From the kitchen a maze of split-level ante-rooms leads to the dining room. Formerly an armoury, this is a magnificent room with high stone arches and small barred windows set into the thick walls. Most of the daylight enters through a nineteenth century fanlight set into the centre of the ceiling and protected by a heavy iron grille against unlawful access from the roof.

A door leads from the dining room into a long, narrow sun lounge, formerly an arched loggia, which overlooks the back garden. It runs parallel to the main façade of the house and has a doorway into the central and most important room in the building; this room may be entered also from the front door at its opposite end. Today the room is used by the family as a drawing room and, occasionally, balls are held in it. Leading off to the right are two large bedrooms and a dressing room through which, down a short flight of stairs, the family passes to the chapel. On the left of the drawing room is another bedroom and a small study, leading to another long, narrow sun lounge overlooking the side garden and courtyard.

The house is now used chiefly in the summer months. Like many other large houses and estates it has become difficult to maintain and run; like many historic survivals, our impatient twentieth century has barely enough time for it.

FORT ST ANGELO

Fort St Angelo stands on one of the main promontories jutting into the blue water of Grand Harbour, facing Valletta. Viewed from the Upper Barracca Gardens, its limestone fortifications, small chapel and old palace can be clearly seen. The first building on the site, however, had a different function. A prehistoric temple was built there more than 1,000 years BC. When the Arabs conquered Malta they pulled down the temple, using some of the stone to build the first castle.

In 1090 Roger the Norman came to Malta and, having got rid of the Arabs, created a small church in the rock itself, dedicating it to the Mother of God. The Chapel of St Anne on the top of the rock, and the old palace, were built in the fifteenth century when governorship of the castle was given to the de Nava family. In the following century the Knights of St John investigated Malta as a possible future home, and their commissioners reported that the island had 'no other defence than a small castle, named St Angelo, which is partly in ruins—its whole artillery consisting of one small cannon, two falcons, and a few iron mortars. . . '

In spite of the island's inadequate defences, the Knights came and the fort was soon extended and strengthened as a protection against the Turks. Six batteries were completed by the time of the Great Siege. The grand master took up residence in de Nava's palace, and the Chapel of St Anne, then used as the Order's chapel, was enlarged. Originally, it was of a simple traditional design, with the customary narrow bays down each side. This was improved by removing every other projecting pier and adding gothic vaults across the remaining bays. Later additions included a south aisle, and an entrance enhanced by a small but elaborately decorated bell-turret. In more recent times the chapel served many purposes, first as an armoury and then as a school; it fell into disuse until 1935, when it was reconsecrated and used as a naval chapel.

The old palace was also improved by the Knights. A winding staircase supported by stone piers was built on the outside of the palace wall, forming a tower with windows cut into it. This type of staircase soon became popular with the Maltese and led to the addition of a second storey to houses, few of which had upper floors at this time. Many underground dungeons and granaries played their part during the Great Siege. One pit, known as the Oubliette, ten feet in diameter, was used as a prison. A carved inscription on the wall complains, in Latin, that the dungeon served as the 'burial place of the living, causing destruction of the good and consolation to the enemy.'

The St Angelo bell also had an important role in the castle's history. The present bell, which bears the date 1716, is part of a strong tradition; at one time sounded as a warning of danger, it now rings only on special festival days.

In the present century St Angelo has not rested on its laurels. In 1912 it was taken over by the Royal Navy as a base ship for

the Mediterranean fleet, instead of the old ship *Egmont*. The fort
became known as HMS *Egmont*, and the commanding officer has
occupied the palace within the fort since that time.

In 1933 the fort was re-named HMS *St Angelo*. The network
of passages under the fortress, extended during the Second World
War, were known as Regent Street, Oxford Street, Petticoat Lane,
and so on. During the war, there were sixty-nine direct hits by
bombs on the castle and much damage was done. The castle, its
wounds healed, now remains a memorial to the two greatest
struggles in Maltese history.

THE MANOEL THEATRE

Despite their turbulent history, the Maltese have usually found
time to enjoy their leisure and today they can point, in Valletta,
to the oldest theatre in the Commonwealth, and one of the oldest
in Europe still in use. Built in 1731 to a design by the French
architect Francois Mondion, it was known first as the Public
Theatre, later as the Theatre Royal and, finally, as the Manoel
Theatre after its founder Antonio Manoel de Vilhena, a Grand
Master of the Knights. He bought for it the site on the corner of
present-day Theatre Street and Old Mint Street, later dedicating
it 'for the honest recreation of the people.' In 1801 an Englishman
who had spent some time in Malta wrote :

> La Valette possesses an opera, small indeed, but neat, though
> much in need of repair. Italy and Sicily supply it with very toler-
> able performances, and it is very agreeable entertainment. It was
> excessively crowded every night by the officers of the expedition,
> to whom it was a source of great amusement. The price of admis-
> sion is one shilling.

Worse times were to befall it. After construction of the larger
opera house in Kingsway, Valletta, in 1866, the theatre was badly
neglected, serving as a haven for beggars who paid a penny a

night to shelter there. In this century it has been used as a dance hall and a cinema, and some people sought refuge there during the bombing raids of the Second World War—one of which demolished the opera house (Plate p. 36). In 1960 the Manoel became a theatre once more, the government of Malta having requisitioned it as the islands' national theatre.

Seen from the street, the façade of the theatre is simple, almost austere, giving no idea of the grandeur within. The main door, centrally placed, is flanked by two smaller doors. These in turn are flanked by two large advertisement panels, above which plain coupled pilasters rise to embrace the upper floors. Over the main door is a long stone balcony with intricately-patterned wrought-iron guard rails. On this balcony, patrons take the air on fine evenings, enjoying a view of the narrow lively street sloping down from Kingsway to Marsamxett harbour.

Seen from the main entrance, the focal point of the auditorium is the fine proscenium arch, framed by Corinthian pilasters, and painted in pale turquoise embellished with gold-decorated shields and palm leaves. The arch leads the eye up to the Vilhena coat of arms which is in the centre under a golden crown. Set into the sides of the arch are the stage boxes, facing each other across the twenty-three-foot proscenium gap and rising from mezzanine level to that of the third tier of boxes in the auditorium. Although these stage boxes do not command a particularly good view of the stage, forty-foot deep, they are the best position from which the magnificent horse-shoe shaped auditorium can be seen.

In the auditorium itself, the boxes follow the curve of the horse-shoe; above the third tier, just below the ceiling, is the gallery. The pit was originally surrounded by boxes, too, but these were later removed to leave two wide curved aisles around either side of the horse-shoe. In the centre of the curve, above the entrance, the governor-general's box commands the best view of the stage. It was from this box that Queen Adelaide watched the performance of Donizetti's *Lucia di Lammermoor* in 1838 and where, more

140

recently, Queen Elizabeth II sat during her state visit to the islands in 1967.

All three tiers of boxes are richly decorated with delicate *paysages* painted in oils on a pale green background, and by mouldings covered with 22-carat gold leaf. Small chandeliers set at intervals add to the splendour. But the ceiling itself is one of the most brilliant features of the auditorium. It is oval in shape, with an oval ventilator grille, decorated and burnished, supporting a magnificent chandelier in the centre. Straight lines running from the oval grille enclose gold-framed turquoise quadrilaterals, increasing in size as the span grows wider towards the edge of the ceiling. Seen from below the effect is almost that of an oval dome, but from the gallery it is clear that the 'dome' is an optical illusion, the ceiling being in fact completely flat.

The wooden stage, relatively new, is surrounded on various levels by a honeycomb of dressing rooms, property rooms, offices and other facilities essential to the running of a modern theatre. After years of change and neglect, therefore, this beautiful building has come once again into its own. Its original character restored, the Manoel Theatre of Valletta can be seen and enjoyed today for what, undoubtedly, it is: a masterpiece of European theatre construction.

THE AUBERGE D'ARAGON

From affairs of pleasure to affairs of state. The Auberge d'Aragon, now the prime minister's official residence and cabinet office, stands on the edge of the Valletta peninsula, facing the Anglican cathedral across the Pjazza Indipendenza. From its windows on the north-west side can be seen the harbour of Marsamxett, Sliema and the blue Mediterranean beyond.

The building, which has served many purposes during its life, was built originally as an *auberge* for the *langue* of Aragon. Standing so near the harbour, it eased the lot of the Knights of

Aragon who had the task of defending one of the bastions at the harbour entrance. It was the first of seven *auberges*, all designed by Gerolamo Cassar. Each is different in scale and style, reflecting the Knights' increase in wealth and Cassar's increase in ingenuity and daring.

The Auberge d'Aragon was begun in 1571 and, being the earliest, is also one of the simplest in layout and design. Distinctly Spanish in appearance, it is rectangular in shape, with a central courtyard or patio and only one main storey. On the north-west side, however, where the street slopes away, there are doors into basement rooms tucked under the building. An ordinary family lives here—co-tenants, as it were, with their prime minister.

The main rooms of the *auberge* intercommunicate and also open into a peristyle surrounding the central patio. Cassar used this basic rectangular plan again in the Auberge d'Italie, but in the other *auberges* not all the sides of the patio are enclosed by main wings of the building. Thus the Auberge de France (now demolished) was an oblong building overlooking a garden at the back.

The façade of the Auberge d'Aragon seen from the *pjazza* is not quite symmetrical. There are three windows on either side of the door, which has a semicircular arch, the Doric portico being a later addition, not by Cassar; complete symmetry was lost because Cassar preferred to put the windows in central positions in the rooms inside and accept a slight external distortion. A greater unity of design is found in some of the later *auberges*. The windows themselves have the 'fat' bulbous-shaped moulding traditionally popular for doors and windows in sixteenth-century Maltese architecture.

In contrast to the façade of the Auberge d'Aragon, the Auberge de Provence (now the National Museum) shows how Cassar's ideas changed and developed. The latter has a rich façade with coupled pillars between each window, alternating triangular and curved pediments on the windows of the first floor, and three

Page 143: Unchanging scene: Sunday morning palaver.

Page 144: Unchanging scene: fields below Mdina

different shapes of window on the ground floor, all exactly symmetrical, the whole being fanciful, rich and balanced to the finest detail. Different again was the design of the Auberge de France where the doorway was far from central, having five large windows edged with Melitan moulding to the left, and two plain windows to the right. These examples suffice to show that the Auberge d'Aragon was the first of a very remarkable series of buildings.

Venturing inside, the main door opens into a barrel-vaulted entrance hall from which marble steps lead up into the peristyle. The wide arches giving onto the rectangular patio have more recently been filled in by a framework containing windows through which the small garden can be seen. One of the doors from the peristyle leads into the present-day cabinet room, which has barrel arches diverging on one side to admit a window. The floor is grey and white marble as in most of the main rooms other than the ballroom. The conference table is surrounded by large leather chairs, and a singular feature is that the smallest, most modest chair is the prime minister's.

The ballroom is a large oblong room with a wooden floor and an arch across the centre with a false pillar on either side. The chestnut beams across the ceiling are similar to the ones in the peristyle but are ornamented with carvings at either end. A frieze in coppery brown and white runs round the room below the carved ends of the beams. Chandeliers light the room, and the furniture includes inlaid cabinets and chairs from France and Sicily.

One of the many intercommunicating doors leads from the ballroom to the reception room, a warm and friendly room in which the prime minister talks with foreign heads of state. The beams across the ceiling are encased and the three regular windows look out across the harbour. Heavy blue-velvet curtains adorn the windows and doors while paintings by Stefano Erardi and Guiseppe Cali (who painted the interior of the Mosta church's vast dome) add colour to the walls. The ornaments include one of the famous seventeenth-century Maltese clocks, its large wooden case painted in many colours; a mosaic of the Madonna, presented by the Pope in 1964; and a casket which is a replica of one built into the wall of the new breakwater in 1904, presented by the Queen in the same year.

On the peristyle walls are the coats of arms of the grand masters and, by the steps to the hall, the old suits of armour. In the *pjazza*'s bright sunlight, this fine old building recalls the opening years of the era of the Knights of St John four centuries ago. Standing as it does in the Square of Independence, with its latest role in Maltese politics, one is reminded also of the hopes and prospects of the new era, the era in which Maltese, at last, are ruled by Maltese.

8   A MODERN VISITOR'S GUIDE

WHILE this book is neither designed nor intended primarily as a guide book, much of the information expected of a guide book may be culled from its pages. For example, chapter 1 contains an impression of Valletta, together with notes on climate and geography; passenger transport facilities, Maltese wines and local handicrafts are mentioned in chapter 6; chapter 7, devoted largely to Maltese architecture, describes half-a-dozen historic buildings in some detail; and so on.

The present chapter is an attempt both to fill in some of the gaps and to provide a general introduction for the intending visitor. But those seeking a full guide-book menu must bear in mind that this chapter is an hors d'oeuvres rather than a main course. More detailed information is obtainable from various books listed in the bibliography, most conveniently perhaps from the guide books by Christopher Kininmonth and Stuart Rossiter; from the admirable *Malta Year Book*; or from publications obtainable free from: Malta Government Tourist Board, 9 Merchants Street, Valletta, Malta, Tel 24444; Malta Government Tourist Office, Malta House, 24 Haymarket, London SW1, Tel 01-839 5033; or from any Maltese embassy, or leading travel agents.

The information given in this chapter is arranged in four parts: what every visitor needs to know, suggestions for the tourist on holiday, notes for students and scholars, and guide lines for visiting business men.

FOR ALL VISITORS
Documents

To enter Malta, citizens of the United Kingdom and Italy need only an identity card. All other nationalities require passports.

147

Visas are not need for a stay of three months or less by visitors from the United Kingdom, Commonwealth countries, west European countries and the United States of America. Certificates of vaccination or innoculation are not needed by visitors from Europe, the USA and Canada.

Currency

Malta is a sterling area country. There are no restrictions on the amounts of currency which may be brought into the islands in notes, travellers' cheques or letters of credit. Maltese currency has the same denominations as British. The same coins are used but the notes are distinctive. Prices in the islands are generally around two-thirds of those prevailing in Britain.

Access

Traditionally there are several direct flights daily between Malta and Britain, Italy and Libya only, with connections at London or Rome to most other countries. Direct flight facilities are being extended gradually over a wider area.

There is no regular UK-Malta service by sea. A small number of passengers are carried by the Prince Line which runs London-Malta-Cyprus-Israel. Summer and winter cruise ships often call at Malta.

There are daily fast train services from London and most European capitals via Rome to Naples, whence it takes less than two days to Malta by regular steamers. These sail about six times monthly, call at Sicilian ports *en route* and continue from Valletta to Tripoli or Benghazi. Alternatively, the train can be taken through to Sicily and passengers can embark there for the shorter (overnight) voyage to Malta. There are car-ferrying facilities from Naples and Sicilian ports. A service by sea between Valletta and Tunis is intended.

Yachts usually report on arrival at the Yacht Marina, Ta Xbiex, in Marsamxett harbour.

148

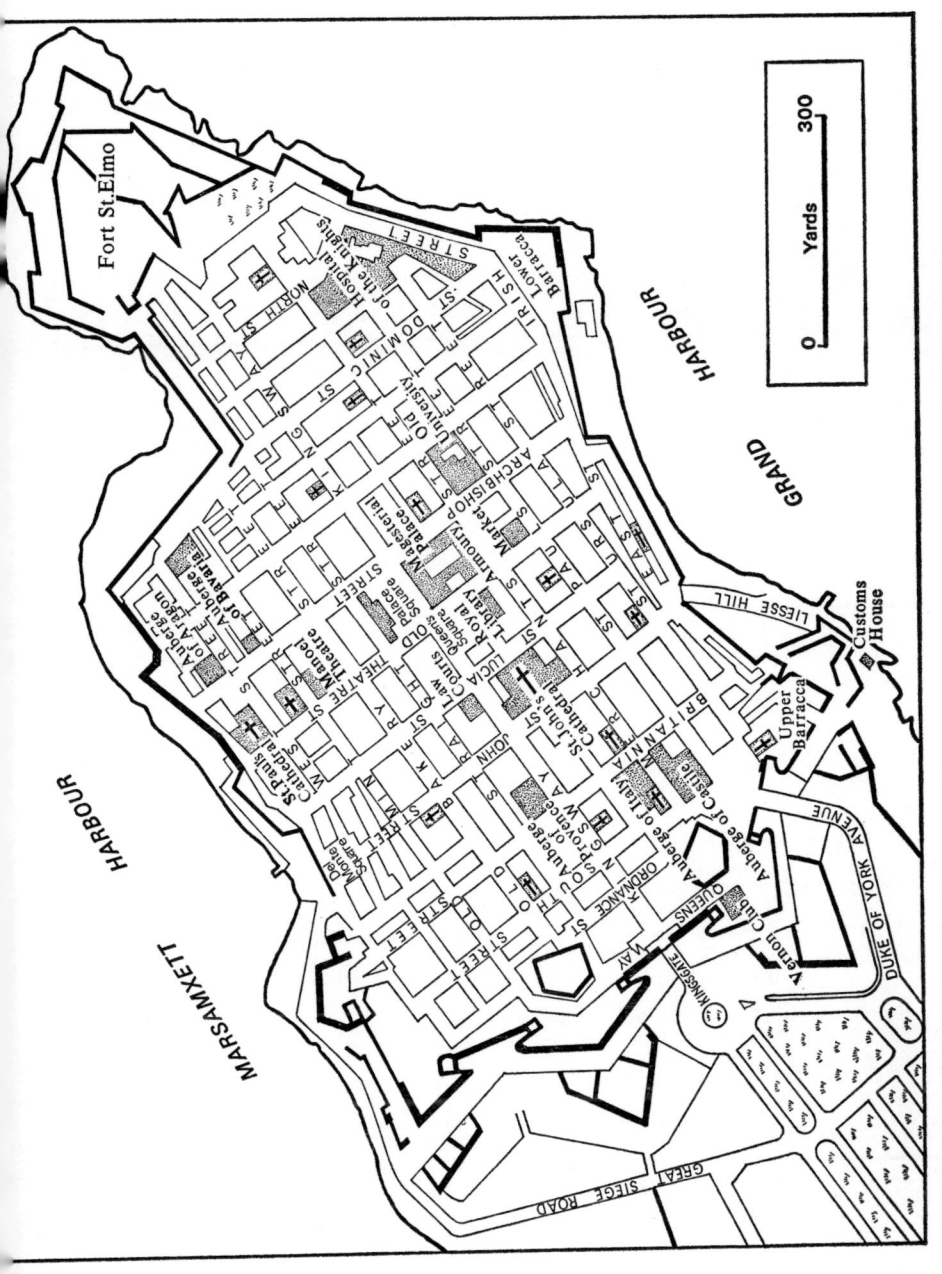

Transport

Bus services radiate to all parts of the main island from two terminuses, Kingsgate and Castile Place, Valletta. Of the small number of cross-country routes, those joining Rabat with Sliema and St Paul's Bay are probably of most interest to visitors. Routes are identified by colours rather than numbers.

There are express connections from Valletta with the ferry from Marfa to Mgarr (Gozo). The ferry runs four to six times daily and has limited accommodation for cars. A fast hydrofoil service connects Valletta (Customs House) with Comino and Gozo.

In Gozo, there is a bus service from Mgarr to Victoria, and thence various rather infrequent services to outlying destinations. The day tripper to Gozo may be well advised to hire a taxi at Mgarr, having negotiated route and price with the driver.

Taxis in the islands have red-and-white number plates. They are equipped with meters but some drivers use their meters with reluctance. In comparison with other services in Malta, taxi charges seem rather high.

Self-drive cars are plentiful and relatively inexpensive. A British or international driving licence is required. Traffic keeps to the left hand side of the road and moves slowly, though angry young men, frustrated by the limitations of their islands' diminutive road system, are apt to break loose and run amok. Officially, there is a strict speed limit on all roads.

Those wishing to go at a gentler pace can hire a *karrozin* for short sight-seeing trips or take a *dghaisa* across the bays and harbours. Fares should be negotiated at the outset.

Accommodation

There are hotels to suit all ages, tastes and pockets in the Maltese Islands, most of them being open the year round. Strangely, however, there is a scarcity of good hotels in Valletta itself, but the well-known Phoenicia, for many years the islands' leading hotel, occupies a fine and convenient position by Kingsgate, just outside the city, and has recently been modernised and enlarged.

The greatest concentration of hotels is to be found in the Sliema-St Julian's conurbation, most of them enjoying water-front positions. In St Julian's, near the Dragonara casino, are the top-category Hilton and Sheraton hotels. In addition, among the better class hotels in the Sliema-St Julian's area offering something special in style or position, are the Cavalieri, Fortina, Imperial, Palms, Preluna, Tigne Court and Villa Rosa. Next in importance as hotel centres are St Paul's Bay and Mellieha. There are hotels of character also in the inland cities and towns of Mdina, San Anton and Victoria (the capital of Gozo).

There is a growing number of modern resort hotels, most of them located alongside the best Maltese bathing beaches, on Gozo and Comino as well as on Malta itself. Most of these are relatively isolated and a few may not open in the winter. In common with most of the larger Maltese hotels, they have swimming pools (in addition to sea bathing, if within reach), full bar and restaurant service, and dancing.

Besides numerous hotels and pensions of more modest category, including a handful in Valletta, there is a large supply of furnished flats and villas which are available on short lets. These are thickest on the ground in the Sliema, St Julian's and St Paul's Bay districts. A prospective tenant in the winter months will be wise to check that adequate heating is provided. Hotels or hostels for students are located in Sliema and St Paul's Bay.

The Malta tourist offices will supply free a descriptive list of hotels (with their prices and facilities) and a list of agents dealing in furnished accommodation.

Food, Drink and Entertainment
The Maltese Islands do not have the reputation of belonging gastronomically in the top league of countries. With the impact

of tourism the standards are improving and, in the smarter hotels and restaurants, an international cuisine can now be enjoyed.

The most pleasant and distinguished place for lunch in or near Valletta is the terrace of the Phoenicia Hotel. The British Hotel has an unpretentious restaurant with commanding views of Grand Harbour. The Cordina and Sacha's are two of Valletta's best restaurants. The Premier Café is a favourite meeting place, indoors or outdoors. Elsewhere in the islands there are few restaurants of note outside the leading hotels, but among the restaurants deserving praise are the Corinthia (San Anton), Casino (Dragonara Point), Buskett Roadhouse (near Rabat), Fondatore and Harbour (St Paul's Bay) and Tunny Net (Mellieha).

The local dishes include *timpana*, a macaroni dish baked in pastry; *lampuki*, a fish pie; stuffed aubergines; and beef olives.

Drinks and cigarettes are relatively inexpensive. The Maltese are substantial consumers of beer and soft drinks; among the latter is the locally-made *Kinnie*, a pleasant bitter-sweet thirst-quencher. Maltese table wines are deservedly popular with visitors, the best-known of them being *Marsovin*, *Lachryma Vitis* and Farmers. A feature of Malta is the large number of small, secluded bars, most of which are open all day until midnight or later. Dancing is a popular pastime and is available in a variety of night spots, ranging from hotel ballrooms through dance halls and open-air terraces to cellars.

There are numerous cinemas showing films in English, but censorship is fairly strict and not every film which achieves fame (or notoriety) in other countries finds its way to the islands' public screens. There are occasional concerts, operas and plays, by visiting or local talent, the Manoel Theatre being the main centre of these activities. The productions of the Malta Amateur Dramatic Club are of a remarkably high standard.

Shops

The main Maltese shopping centres are in Valletta and Sliema.

In the former city the shops are mostly concentrated in or near Kingsway, the main thoroughfare, whereas in Sliema they tend to be scattered among the various neighbourhoods. Shops are generally open every weekday between 9 am and 8 pm with a two-hour lunch break. Banks open only in the mornings. On Sunday one chemist remains open in each town or village.

Festivals

Of interest to most visitors are the numerous religious or national *festas*, with colourful processions, bands, fireworks and illuminations. One important celebration is that of St Paul's shipwreck on 10 February. At Carnival time—the week before Lent —people wear masks and attend fancy-dress balls and processions; on Good Friday the tone is more solemn although there is much colourful pageantry in the streets. The Feast of St Peter and St Paul on June 28-29, known as the *Imnarja*, is held at night; it is the traditional Maltese feast of folk music, singing and dancing, with street races on bare-backed horses and donkeys.

National Day on 8 September commemorates both the victory over the Turks in the sixteenth century and the lifting of the 'greater' siege in the Second World War, and on this occasion water events in Grand Harbour are a main attraction. Independence Day is celebrated on 21 September with parades and bands in Floriana and Valletta. In all, there are fifteen annual public holidays and some fifty *festas*, most of the latter being local events involving one town or village at a time.

FOR THE TOURIST

Ancient Sites

There are many well-preserved prehistoric sites in the islands, of which the most spectacular include the Ggantija temples in Gozo, the Hagar Qim near Qrendi, the Hypogeum catacombs in

Paola and the complex of temples at Tarxien. There are important Roman remains in Rabat.

Places of Interest in or near Valletta

St John's Co-Cathedral.

The Grand Master's Palace and Armoury.

The surviving *auberges*, particularly those of Aragon (chapter 7) and Castile; also

The National Museum, formerly the Auberge of Provence.

The Manoel Theatre (chapter 7).

The General Post Office, formerly the Parisio Palace.

Queen's Square, for its open-air café, the passing scene, and some adjacent features including the Royal Malta Library, Palace Square, arcaded shops and street markets.

The Barracca gardens for panoramic views of Grand Harbour.

The Fort St Elmo vantage points.

The Customs House.

The Porte des Bombes in Floriana.

Fort St Angelo (chapter 7) and remains of the earlier *auberges* in Vittoriosa.

The yacht marina at Ta Xbiex.

Other Places of Interest

Mdina—the cathedral (chapter 7), old houses and narrow streets.

The casino at Dragonara Point, near St Julian's.

San Anton gardens.

The church in Mosta with its spectacular dome.

The Blue Grotto.

Calypso's Cave, in Gozo.

Views

The harbour creeks and bays, from the waterside roads connecting Valletta, Ta Xbiex, Sliema and St Julian's.

The coastline, from the road between St Julian's and St Paul's Bay.

Hilly countryside between St Paul's Bay and Mellieha.

Gozo, from terraces near the church in Mellieha.

Gozo and its capital city, from Gran Castello in Victoria.

Mdina, from the approach road below Rabat; also, the countryside from the Mdina bastions.

Cliffs near Dingli.

Tour of the Harbours

A delightful way to view Valletta's fortifications from the water. The trip, which takes in most of the roadsteads and creeks of Grand and Marsamxett harbours, starts at Sliema and lasts about two hours.

Swimming

Sea bathing may be enjoyed from May to October, with an average water temperature of 74F. The best and biggest beaches are at the north-west end of the main island. There is enjoyable rock bathing at many places in all three islands. Conditions and facilities for all water sports are excellent, five of the leading centres being Dragonara, St George's Bay, St Paul's Bay, Mellieha Bay and Comino. There is a large open-air swimming pool and lido on Dragonara Point.

Sailing

There are regular races in the season for cruising and dinghy classes. Sea-going picnics and bathing parties, combined with visits to the less-frequented bay and beaches, are a favourite hot-weather pastime. Yachts and dinghies may be hired by visitors.

Other Sport

The national sport is soccer and the leading Maltese teams are

155

very competent. Marsa is the main centre for golf, polo, tennis, squash, and horse racing. There is a modern bowling-alley at Gzira.

FOR THE SCHOLAR AND STUDENT

Museums and Libraries
 National Museum, Valletta.
 Royal Malta Library, Valletta.
 Roman Museum, Rabat.
 Cathedral Museum, Mdina.
 Bird Museum, Naxxar.
 Botanic Gardens, Floriana.
 Gozo Museum, Victoria.
 Other museums are located at various ancient sites, including those listed in part two.

Student facilities
 There are short courses in various subjects for visitors, notably archaeology, history, architecture, art, drama, music and folklore. There are guided tours for students to ancient sites and historic buildings. Arrangements can be made for students to spend a day with a Maltese family. Sponsors include the National Students Travel Service, St Paul's Street, Valletta; the British Council, Pjazza Indipendenza, Valletta; and the Hotel International Student Centre, Bugibba, St Paul's Bay. Holders of a recognised student card can enjoy various sports at reduced prices.

Flora and Fauna
 Among the trees and shrubs to be found in the islands are 'the hardy and indigenous' carob, prickly pear, olive, bay, almond, fig, pomegranate, pine, oak, tamarisk, thyme, vine, orange and lemon. Wild flowers of many varieties, mostly Italian types, carpet the hills and fields in the spring. Local creatures include rabbit, hedgehog, bat, frog, lizard, green snake and, on the wing, lark, plover,

sparrow, thrush and a small range of sea birds. There is also a distinctive Maltese breed of dog.

FOR THE BUSINESS VISITOR

Sources of Information or Introduction

An enquirer wishing to identify the appropriate Maltese government department should seek guidance from the Government Information Service, 24 Merchants Street, Valletta, telephone 24901. This office can also supply a complete list of official publications.

Industrialists who have in mind opening a plant or factory in the islands, and businessmen seeking outlets for trade and investments, may find in the following select list of organisations (Valletta-based, unless otherwise stated) the point of contact they need:

Government:
   Ministry of Finance, Customs and Port
   Ministry of Trade, Industry and Agriculture
   Ministry of Education and Tourism
Industry and Trade:
   Malta Development Corporation
   Federation of Malta Industries
   Chamber of Commerce
Banks:
   The chief banks, with branches throughout the islands, are the National Bank of Malta, the Government Savings Bank and Barclays Bank DCO.
   The Malta Trade Fair offices are at Naxxar.
   The leading English-language newspaper is *The Times of Malta.*
   The British High Commissioner's office is at 7 St Anne's Street, Floriana.

The principal social clubs are the Casino Maltese (not to be confused with the casino at Dragonara Point, whose main purpose is gambling) and the Union Club in Sliema. Other clubs of distinction include the United Services Sports Club at Marsa, the Royal Malta Yacht Club at Pieta, the Overseas League and the Anglo-Maltese League.

Business laws, ethics and methods are much the same as in Britain. The Maltese, being kindly people, are patient and good-humoured with visitors, but it would be unwise to construe their easy manners as a cloak for lack of drive or acumen. The Maltese are shrewd, tenacious and well-informed in business negotiation and—as their history has shown often enough—it can prove costly to under-rate them.

9   INTO THE FUTURE

THE Maltese Islands are at a stage of development, with few clear signposts to point the way, when it is perhaps easier to ask questions about this new nation's future than to answer them.

In the early years from 1964, when independence was won, Borg Olivier's nationalist party provided stable and progressive government. On the whole, this was a period of growing momentum, of reaching forward towards a new and challenging future, and it could be several more years before the tempo slackens. Thus, for the time being, changes of government are unlikely to be the cause of any marked deviation in national policies or purposes. However, alterations of emphasis or pace, in both foreign and domestic affairs, will be evident with Dom Mintoff's labour party in office, and with the two main parties commanding roughly equal support amongst Maltese voters, changes of government and a lively political atmosphere are undoubtedly to be expected.

In foreign affairs the most critical decisions for the islands are concerned with defence relationships. There exist in Malta various operational and training base facilities, attractive to foreign powers, which are a source of income and, to some extent, of employment for the Maltese. The question is : with which foreign power or combination of powers is it in the best interests of the Maltese to associate? On the face of it, if Britain is withdrawing effectively from the Mediterranean, the choice seems to lie between NATO, which already has modest facilities in Malta, and Russia, whose growing naval presence is the new and dominant strategic factor in that region.

There are some Maltese in positions of influence who, having

159

missed their vocation as tight-rope walkers, would like to start a flirtation with the Russian bears, assuming that passionate hugs may be avoided before intentions have been gauged. While this could be one way to raise the bidding by western suitors, it would be unfortunate if the gamble were to fail and the Maltese, having so recently gained their freedom, enter unwittingly into a new state of vassalage. The Maltese people should decide unequivocally whether their lot lies with the west, with the east, or, neutrally, with neither.

Alas, for a small defenceless nation dependent on international status and trade for its livelihood, neutrality almost certainly means decline. Is there no other 'middle' way? One idea that has been mooted is that the Maltese might offer base facilities to a loose association of four or five friendly countries which between them, while contributing in this way to Maltese prosperity, would guarantee the islands' security. At first, the eligible countries might comprise Britain, Italy, France and, conceivably, Tunisia and Libya. The issues involved in this arrangement are undoubtedly complicated and, if the Maltese elect to remain under the NATO umbrella, this may be in the long run the best as well as the easiest solution.

INDUSTRY AND INFLATION

Official policy for the development of new industry places emphasis on those enterprises which are 'male labour-intensive, export-oriented, with low raw material costs.' This is sound but cannot be applied inflexibly. Already there are shortages of male labour in branches of the tourism and construction industries with, at the same time, fairly substantial unemployment in some trades and a high emigration rate. An urgent need is to re-train and re-deploy sizeable elements of the existing Maltese labour force.

But industry and commerce are growing—or should soon be growing—at a fast enough pace to absorb available male workers *and* a rising proportion of newly-recruited female labour. As the old order crumbles, social disciplines are weakening and, with the increasing emancipation of women, more jobs will have to be provided for them whether the authorities like it or not. This trend will accelerate. Maltese workers and their families, influenced by television and by the impression of affluence conveyed by tourism, will soon expect better houses and more possessions to go with them. Already, in a land where nowhere is more than two score miles by road from anywhere, the two-car family is becoming a middle-class characteristic. Young people, better-educated and better-paid, are creating new demands for consumer goods. All these appetites will have to be satisfied and the larger household bills paid, and this inevitably means more women going out to work.

It may also mean creeping inflation and, later, higher taxation. Wages rise so costs rise so prices rise so wages rise . . .; in other countries, it is a familiar story. On balance, despite increasing imports, the proportion of inland revenue from customs dues will probably fall and, to meet the higher costs of improved social services, other forms of taxation will have to yield more.

In industry, however, the critical long-term problem is one of scale. As rising standards of living and inflationary pressures reduce the wage advantage at present enjoyed by Maltese industry, the emphasis must be increasingly on greater efficiency and higher productivity. This means the application of modern management-techniques in plants large enough to deploy them. The need is urgent, for Maltese industry, faced inescapably with the cost of shipping raw materials in and finished goods out, lacks a tradition of industrial management. Hitherto, the authorities have been slow in coming to terms with this serious gap in their armoury of industrial weapons. While new education and training facilities for management trainees are gradually being provided, the problem is largely one of attitude-changing. Will those who own and finance and influence industry in the islands think big enough, soon enough?

More particularly, it is to be expected that saturation may be reached in the early 1970s in the key Maltese construction, tourism and, possibly, textile industries. In view of power and water limitations, among other factors, it seems probable that efficient precision-working industries—in the light engineering, hydraulic and electronic fields—and mechanical assembly industries will form the main export-oriented growth sector of manufacturing industry; while firms producing for home consumption will also have to be highly competent. Impressive pace-setters in both categories are already making their mark—for example, in printing and flour milling.

Unfortunately many problems, both of marketing and manning in Malta's dry docks, remain to be solved. Closure of the Suez Canal dealt a serious blow to this important enterprise, though blame for most of its ills lies in restrictive attitudes and practices which have not been abandoned quickly enough. The militancy of the General Workers' Union has not always been well calculated.

MAKING ENDS MEET

If the Maltese Islands are to become industrially a miniature 'Switzerland' of the Mediterranean, this could be even more aptly the case in trade and finance. Invisible trade could be much further stimulated than was envisaged in the first two five-year plans, and contribute more towards solution of the balance-of-payments problem. Valletta is well poised to become a centre of commercial development in banking, insurance and investment. The proposed free-port venture, and the tax inducements available both to incoming industry and to approved immigrants, are part of the pattern. And so, for example, is the yacht marina, with its berths for 1,500 yachts and supporting infra structure.

But a most important catalyst, both in Valletta's development

162

as a financial centre, and generally in this new nation's quest for assured maturity, will be the new stock exchange. Under careful supervision by the recently-established Central Bank, working closely with the Development Corporation, the stock exchange could be the greatest single factor in achieving what Lord Robens has called 'an economically self-propelled society'. For, once confidence is established in the new exchange, much of the capital now hoarded or invested abroad will flow into Valletta, and the Maltese, to an important extent, will no longer be dependent on foreign financiers. It may be some while before equity shares in local public companies can be marketed, but interesting opportunities for investment ought to become available in the near future in public utilities, in preference stock and through the Development Corporation's holdings in companies whose expansion projects have received official blessing.

In general, it may be expected that the Maltese people will reach a watershed in their affairs in 1975. British financial support is due to have ended by then and, committed to established or developing programmes—political, social, economic and industrial —the choice of roads ahead will be limited. Much of the novelty of being a newly-independent nation will have worn off. There may be more acrimony in politics and possibly in industrial relations, particularly if present decisions have failed to stand the test of time, and the boom of the early seventies has begun to level out.

The key question, it seems, is whether the Maltese will by then have achieved, or be in sight of, a balanced economy. At the time of writing, there is quite a long way to go towards this goal. On the other hand, most of the early steps seem to have been well and carefully chosen. Morale is high. The people have the bonus of political stability, a good sense of social justice, high educational standards and a progressive outlook. The islanders are fortunate in being a close-knit community, with a long history of mutual give-and-take. Religious and industrious, they know how to cope with difficult times, and their country occupies a geographical position which, for one reason or another, will continue to be attractive to the outsider. Above all, the Maltese believe in their future and there can be no dynamic element of greater significance than that.

APPENDIXES

APPENDIX A

MILESTONES AND RULERS

167

1557	Jean Parisot de la Valette
1568	Pietro del Monte
1572	Jean l'Evêque de la Cassière
1581	Hugues Loubenx de Verdalle
1595	Martin Garzes
1601	Alof de Wignacourt
1622	Luiz Mendez de Vasconcellos
1623	Antoine de Paule
1636	Jean Paul de Lascaris Castellar
1657	Martin de Redin
1660	Annet de Clermont de Chattes Gessan
1660	Rafael Cotoner
1663	Nicolas Cotoner
1680	Gregorio Carafa
1690	Adrien de Wignacourt
1697	Ramon Perellos y Roccaful
1720	Marc'Antonio Zondadari
1722	Antonio Manoel de Vilhena
1736	Ramon Despuig
1741	Manoel Pinto de Fonseca
1773	Francisco Ximenes de Texada
1775	Emmanuel de Rohan Polduc
1797	Ferdinand von Hompesch

Civil Commissioners

1799	Captain Alexander Ball RN
1801	Sir Charles Cameron
1802	Rear-Admiral Sir Alexander Ball
1810	Lt-General Sir Hildebrand Oakes

Governors

1813	Lt-General the Hon Sir Thomas Maitland
1824	General the Marquess of Hastings

1827	Major-General the Hon Sir Frederic Ponsonby
1836	Lt-General Sir Henry Bouverie
1843	Lt-General Sir Patrick Stuart
1847	The Right Hon Richard More O'Ferrall
1851	Major-General Sir William Reid
1858	Lt-General Sir John Gaspard le Marchant
1864	Lt-General Sir Henry Storks
1867	General Sir Patrick Grant
1872	General Sir Charles Van Straubenzee
1878	General Sir Arthur Borton
1884	General Sir Lintern Simmonds
1888	Lt-General Sir Henry Torrens
1890	Lt-General Sir Henry Smyth
1893	General Sir Arthur Fremantle
1899	Lt-General Lord Grenfell
1903	General Sir Mansfield Clarke
1907	Lt-General Sir Henry Grant
1909	General Sir Leslie Rundle
1915	Field Marshal Lord Methuen
1919	Field Marshal Viscount Plumer
1924	General Sir Walter N. Congreve vc
1927	General Sir John du Cane
1931	General Sir David Campbell
1936	General Sir Charles Bonham-Carter
1940	Lt-General Sir William Dobbie
1942	Field Marshal Viscount Gort vc
1944	Lt-General Sir Edmond Schreiber
1946	Sir Francis (later Lord) Douglas
1949	Sir Gerald Creasy
1954	Major General Sir Robert Laycock
1959	Admiral Sir Guy Grantham
1962	Sir Maurice Dorman

APPENDIX A

Prime Ministers

1921	Joseph Howard
1923	Francesco Buhagiar
1924	Sir Ugo P. Mifsud
1927	Sir Gerald Strickland
1932	Sir Ugo P. Mifsud (to 1933)
1947	Dr (later Sir) Paul Boffa
1949	Dom Mintoff
1950	Dr Enrico Mizzi
1950	Dr George Borg Olivier
1955	Dom Mintoff
1962	Dr George Borg Olivier

APPENDIX B

PRINCIPAL FEAST DAYS

*1 January**	New Year's Day
*6 January**	Epiphany
*10 February**	St Paul's Shipwreck
Week before Lent	Carnival
*19 March**	St Joseph
Friday before Palm Sunday	Our Lady of Sorrows—Valletta
*Good Friday**	
*1 May**	St Joseph the Worker
*Ascension Day**	
5th Sunday after Easter	St Publius, first Bishop of Malta
Trinity Sunday	Holy Trinity
*Corpus Christi**	
24 June	St John the Baptist
*29 June**	St Peter and St Paul (Imnarja)
16 July	Our Lady of Mount Carmel— Valletta
3rd Sunday in July	Our Lady of Mount Carmel— Mdina
Last Sunday in July	Our Lady of Sorrows—St Paul's Bay
*15 August**	Assumption
Sunday before last Sunday in August	Our Lady Star of the Sea—Sliema

171

APPENDIX B

*8 September**	Our Lady of Victories
*21 September**	Independence Day
*1 November**	All Saints
*8 December**	Immaculate Conception
*25 December**	Christmas Day

Public holidays

APPENDIX C

CLIMATIC TABLE

Month	Sun (hours)	Rain (inches)	Temperature range (Fahrenheit)
January	5.2	3.2	63–46
February	5.6	2.2	64–47
March	7.0	1.6	68–48
April	8.7	0.9	72–51
May	10.0	0.4	78–56
June	11.6	0.1	85–63
July	12.5	0.05	92–69
August	11.6	0.2	91–70
September	9.1	1.2	86–69
October	7.2	3.0	82–63
November	5.6	3.4	74–54
December	5.1	3.8	67–49

APPENDIX D

MALTESE ALPHABET

Maltese	*English*
a	a
b	b
c	hard c
ċ	ch
d	d
e	e
f	f
g	hard g
ġ	j
gh	virtually inaudible
h	sometimes silent, sometimes aspirated
i	i
j	y
k	k
l	l
m	m
n	n
o	o
p	p
q	weakly gurgled k
r	r
s	s
t	t
u	u
v	v
w	w
x	sh
ż	tz
z	z

BIBLIOGRAPHY

Part One: Books in alphabetical sequence of author

ALLEN, J. H. *A Pictorial Tour in the Mediterranean*. London, 1843

ANGAS, G. F. *A Ramble in Malta and Sicily*. London, 1842

ATCHISON, THOMAS. *Trial of Captain Thomas Atchison*. London, 1825

ATCHISON, THOMAS. *Petition to the King*. London, 1829

AZZOPARDI-SANT, EDWARD. *Malta, A Shock of Delight*. Malta, 1931

BADGER, G. PERCY. *Description of Malta and Gozo*. Malta, 1838

BADGER, G. PERCY. *Historical Guide to Malta*. Malta, 1879

BALLOU, MATURIN M. *The Story of Malta*. Boston, USA, 1893

BARTLETT, W. H. *Gleanings Pictorial and Antiquarian on the Overland Route*. London, 1851

BARTOLO, AUGUSTO. *Malta, A Neglected Outpost of Empire: some plain speaking*. Malta, 1911

BARTOLO, AUGUSTO. *The Sovereignty of Malta and the Nature of its Title*. Malta, 1909

BEDFORD, THE REV W. K. R. *Gleanings from Malta*. London, 1880

BEDFORD, THE REV W. K. R. *Malta from an Englishman's Point of View*. London, 1892

BELLANTI, P. F. *Studies in Maltese History*. Malta, 1924

BEELEY, BRIAN W. *A Bibliography of the Maltese Islands*. Durham University, 1959

BENNETT, J. H. *Winter and Spring on the Shores of the Mediterranean*. London, 1875

BIGELOW, ANDREW. *Travels in Malta and Sicily in 1827*. Boston, USA, 1831

BLAQUIERE, E. *Letters from the Mediterranean*. London, 1813

BIBLIOGRAPHY

BLOUET, BRIAN. *The Story of Malta*. London, 1967; published as; *A Short History of Malta*. New York, 1967

BOISGELIN, LOUIS DE. *Ancient and Modern Malta*. London, 1804

BOISSEVAIN, JEREMY. *Maltese Village Politics*. London, 1961

BOISSEVAIN, JEREMY. *Saints and Fireworks: Religion and Politics in Rural Malta*. London, 1965

BOURNE, H. R. F. *Malta*. London, 1879

BOWEN-JONES, H., DEWDNEY, J. C., FISHER, W. B. *Malta—Background for Development*. Durham University, 1961

BRADFORD, ERNLE. *The Great Siege*. London and New York, 1962

BRADLEY, ROBERT NOEL. *Malta and the Mediterranean Race*. London, 1912

BRAUN, H. *An Introduction to Maltese Architecture*. Malta, 1944

BROCKMAN, ERIC. *The Last Bastion*. London, 1961

BROWN, EDWARD. *Travels and Adventures of Edward Brown Esq.* London, 1739

BRYANS, ROBIN. *Malta and Gozo*. London, 1966

BRYDONE, PATRICK. *A Tour through Sicily and Malta*. London, 1773

CASOLANI, C. *The Sanitary Question in Malta*. Malta, 1880

CHURCHILL, WINSTON S. *The Second World War*. Vols 3 and 4. London, 1950, 1951

CIRILLO, THE REV R. *Report on the Social Aspects of Maltese Agriculture*. Malta, 1959

CLARK, CUMBERLAND. *Crown Colonies and their History*. London, 1939

COCKBURN, GENERAL SIR GEORGE. *A Voyage to Cadiz and Gibraltar, Sicily and Malta*. London, 1815

COLLINS, FRANCIS. *Voyages 1796-1801*. London, 1807

CREMONA, J. J. *The Malta Constitution of 1835 and its Historic Background*. Malta, 1959

CREMONA, J. J. *An Outline of the Constitutional Development of Malta under British Rule*. Malta, 1963

CRITIEN, L. *Guide to Malta and its Dependencies*. Malta, 1888

CROCKES, H. E. *History of the Fortifications of Malta*. Malta, 1920

DARMANIN, J. F. *Fort St Angelo.* Malta, 1948

DAVY, JOHN. *Notes and Observations on the Ionian Islands and Malta.* London, 1842

DE NON, BARON DOMINIQUE VIVANT. *Travels in Sicily and Malta.* London, 1789

DOBBIE, SYBIL. *Grace under Malta.* London, 1943

DOMEIER, W. *Observations on the Climate, Manners and Amusements of Malta.* London, 1810

ETON, WILLIAM. *Authentic Materials for a History of the People of Malta.* London, 1802

ETON, WILLIAM. *Appeals for a free Constitution.* Malta, 1811

EVANS, G. H. *Guide to Malta and Gozo.* Portsmouth, 1914

EVANS, J. D. *Malta.* London, 1959

GALEA, R. V. *Architecture in Malta.* Malta, 1914

GALT, JOHN. *Voyages and Travels in the years 1809, 1810 and 1811.* London, 1812

GODWIN, THE REV G. N. *A Guide to the Maltese Islands.* Malta, 1880

GRIFFITHS, W. A. *A Brief Outline of the Foundation and Development of HM Naval Establishment at Malta.* London, 1917

HARDIMAN, W. *A History of Malta 1798-1815.* London, 1909

HERAUD, JOHN A. *Voyages up the Mediterranean and in the Indian Seas.* London, 1837

HOARE, SIR RICHARD COLT. *A Classical Tour.* London, 1819

HUGHES, QUENTIN. *Fortress: Architecture and Military History in Malta.* London, 1969

JACKSON, JOHN. *Reflections on Commerce of the Mediterranean.* London, 1804

KININMONTH, CHRISTOPHER. *Travellers' Guide to Malta and Gozo.* London, 1967

LAFERLA, A. V. *Story of Man in Malta.* Malta, 1935

LAFERLA, A. V. *British Malta.* Malta, 1947

LANFRANCO, GUIDO G. *The Fishes of Malta.* Malta, 1965

LANFRANCO, GUIDO G. *The Flora of Malta.* Malta, 1965

LEWIS, SIR G. C. *Life and Letters.* London, 1870

L

BIBLIOGRAPHY

LUKE, SIR HARRY. *Malta, An Account and Appreciation*. London, 1949

LUTTMAN-JOHNSON, LT COL FREDERICK. *A Handbook to Malta for all ranks of both Services*. Malta, 1899

MACGILL, T. *Handbook or guide for Strangers visiting Malta*. Malta, 1839

MACKINNON, THE REV A. G. T. *Malta, the Nurse of the Mediterranean*. London, 1916

MACMILLAN, ALLISTER. *Malta and Gibralter*. London, 1915

MACMUNN, N. E. *Malta*. Oxford, 1914

MALCOLM, ALEXANDER. *Letters of an Invalid from Italy and Malta*. London, 1897

MANDUCA, JOHN. *Tourist Guide to Malta and Gozo*. Malta, 1967

MIEGE, M. *Histoire de Malte*. Paris, 1840

MITROVICH, GEORGE. *The Claims of the Maltese*. London, 1835

MITROVICH, GEORGE. *The Cause of the People of Malta*. London, 1836

MIZZI, M. A. M. *Voice from Malta*. Malta, 1896

MONK, WINSTON F. *Britain in the Western Mediterranean*. London, 1953

MONSON, W. J. *Extracts from a Journal*. London, 1820

OWEN, CHARLES. *Britons Abroad*. London, 1968

PANZAVECCIA, FORTUNATO. *A Short History of Malta*. Malta, 1849

PAPPAFFY, GIOVANNI DI NICOLO. *The Merchants and the Currency of Malta*. Malta, 1851

PETO, G. E. *Malta and Cyprus*. London, 1927

PORTER, MAJOR WHITWORTH. *A History of the Fortress of Malta*. Malta, 1858

REYNOLDS-BALL, EUSTACE A. *Mediterranean Winter Resorts*. London, 1899

RITCHIE, CAPTAIN LEWIS. *The Epic of Malta*. London, 1943

ROBERTS, E. L. *The Birds of Malta*. Malta, 1954

ROSE, HAROLD. *Your Guide to Malta*. London, 1963

ROSSITER, STUART. *The Blue Guide to Malta*. London, 1968

178

RYAN, F. W. *Travels.* London, 1910

SAMMUT, DR EDWARD. *Notes for a History of Art in Malta.* Malta, 1954

SANKEY, FRANCIS F. *Malta considered with reference to its eligibility as a place of residence for invalids.* London, 1849

SEDDALL, THE REV HENRY. *Malta: Past and Present.* London, 1870

SHANKLAND, PETER; HUNTER, ANTHONY. *Malta Convoy.* London, 1961

SITWELL, SACHEVERELL; ARMSTRONG-JONES, TONY. *Malta.* London, 1958

SLADE, ADOLPHUS. *Turkey, Greece and Malta.* London, 1837

SMITH, PROF HARRISON. *The British in Malta.* Malta, 1953

STRICKLAND, SIR GERALD. *India and Malta: a Parallel.* London, 1934

TALLACK, WILLIAM. *Malta under the Phoenicians, Knights and English.* London, 1861

WALSH, THOMAS. *Journal of the Late Campaign in Egypt.* London, 1803

WEBSTER, W. B. *English Governors and Foreign Grumblers.* London, 1864

WIGNACOURT, JOHN. *The Odd Man in Malta.* London, 1914

WILKINSON, CHARLES. *Epitome of the History of Malta and Gozo.* London, 1804

WILSON, THE REV SAMUEL S. *A narrative of the Great Mission: or Sixteen Years in Malta and Greece.* London, 1839

WOOD, SIR MARK. *The Importance of Malta considered in 1796 and 1798.* London, 1803

ZAMMIT, SIR THEMISTOCLES. *Malta, The Islands and their History.* Malta, 1929

Part Two: Other publications and periodicals

BATTELLE MEMORIAL INSTITUTE : *Battelle Survey.* 1963

BROADCASTING AUTHORITY : *Annual Report for 1966-7.* Malta, 1967

BIBLIOGRAPHY

COMMERCE, CHAMBER OF : *Century of Progress 1848-1948*. Malta

GEOGRAPHICAL MAGAZINE : *Island in Transition* by Charles Owen. London, July 1966

HMS ST ANGELO : *A brief History of Fort St Angelo*. Malta, 1967

HMSO : *Air Battle of Malta*. London, 1944

HMSO : *Malta*. London, 1964

HMSO : *Reference pamphlet 63, and supplement Malta: Independence Constitution 1964*. London, 1964

HMSO : *Commonwealth Development and its Financing, No 10*. London, 1966

INDUSTRY, DEPARTMENT OF : *Manufacturing in Malta*. Malta, 1964

INDUSTRY, DEPARTMENT OF : *Manufacturers and Exporters 1968*. Malta, 1968

INFORMATION, DEPARTMENT OF : *Review of the Development Plan for the Maltese Islands 1959-64*. Malta, 1961

INFORMATION, DEPARTMENT OF : *Development Plan for the Maltese Islands 1964-69*. Malta, 1964

INFORMATION, DEPARTMENT OF : *Budget Speech*. Malta, 1966

INFORMATION, DEPARTMENT OF : *Joint Mission for Malta (The Robens Report.)* Malta, 1967

INFORMATION, DEPARTMENT OF : *Malta in brief*. Malta, 1968

MALTA TODAY : *Aids to Industries Board and the Industrial Development Board*. Malta, January 1967

MALTA TODAY : *From Crafts to Industries*. Malta, July 1967

MARKETING RESEARCH DEPARTMENT : *Malta, an Economic Brief*. Malta, 1964 and 1965

MELITA HISTORICA : *The Influence of Italian Mannerism upon Maltese Architecture* by Quentin Hughes. Malta, 1952

MELITA HISTORICA : *Development of the Malta Constitution* by Hilda Lee. Malta, 1952

MELITA HISTORICA : *British Policy towards Religion* by Hilda Lee. Malta, 1964

SCOTTISH GEOGRAPHICAL MAGAZINE : *Notes on Rural Malta* by J. B. Fleming. September 1946

BIBLIOGRAPHY

SOCIAL SERVICES, DEPARTMENT OF : *Report*. Malta, 1966

SUNDAY TIMES MAGAZINE : *Alamein and the Desert War*. London, 17 September 1967

TIMES OF MALTA : *The Land Steamer—Malta's Railway*. Malta, 19 February 1963

TOURIST BOARD : *Architecture, Painting and Sculpture*. Malta, 1967

TOURIST BOARD : *Malta*. Malta, 1967

UNITED NATIONS : *Economic Adaptation and Development in Malta. (The Stolper Report)*. 1964

and

The Malta Year Book published annually by St Michael's College Publications, Malta.

ACKNOWLEDGMENTS

When I began work on this book the Maltese Islands were already quite well known to me, my latest of several visits having been in 1966 to gather material for an article for the *Geographical Magazine*. I have since had the pleasure of five more visits, and the better I get to know the islands the more I love them. Thus, despite a lot of tiresome research work at the preparatory stages, writing this book has been no hardship.

Research in Malta took three forms: interviewing people, going places, and studying a great deal of published material. Among those whom I mined most deeply for local leads and information were my friends Ian Cox (who supplied the piece about wine in chapter 6), Joseph Galea (who vetted the historical chapters), Joe Micallef (who gave me valuable introductions) and Joan Parker (who contributed the description of the Manoel Theatre in chapter 7). Others who also gave freely of their time included Baroness Testaferrata Abela (who provided information about Gomerino for chapter 7), Ba Amato, Father Anthony Borg (who supplied the description of the Gozitan church in chapter 7), Victor Denaro, Sir Hannibal Scicluna, and Ella and Kay Warren.

Useful discussions were held with senior officials of several government and public bodies in Valletta, notably of the Tourist Board (who went out of their way repeatedly to be helpful and attentive), the Department of Information (also friendly and co-operative beyond the call of duty), the Ministry of Trade, Industry and Agriculture, the Malta Development Corporation, the British Council, Barclays Bank and, by no means least, the charmingly housed and welcoming Chamber of Commerce. Others who kindly helped with advice or information were Baron Testaferrata Bonici, Professor Salvino Busuttil, Father Maurice Grech, Colonel

183

ACKNOWLEDGMENTS

Frank Cassar Torregiana and (in England) Captain Errol Turner.

As my bibliography implies, there was much poring over books and other publications. I am grateful to Rosemary Ratcliff and Helen Doyle whose diligent researches were to an important extent the basis of chapters 2 and 3 and of chapters 5, 6 and 7 respectively. I should like to acknowledge also the willing co-operation of Doctor V. A. Depasquale and his assistants at the Royal Malta Library in Valletta; and, in London, of D. H. Simpson and his staff at the Royal Commonwealth Society and of the library staffs at the British Museum and the London Library.

All except three of the photographs appearing in this book were supplied free by the Tourist Board in Valletta, several being taken specially to meet my needs. This helpful gesture is greatly appreciated. My wife, Felicity, besides offering encouragement at various stages, checked and compiled the bibliography—a true labour of love. My thanks are due also to Angela Evans and Catherine Skinner for typing most of the manuscript. The index, prepared when the book was in proof, was the work of Susan Bailey, whose prompt assistance I gladly acknowledge.

INDEX

185

189

INDEX